Love Yourself Into Your Best Life!

HOW ANYONE IN MIDLIFE CAN MASTER SELF-LOVE AND ENHANCE RELATIONSHIPS FOR LASTING HAPPINESS

JILLIAN BEANNE

Contents

Introduction

Have you ever found yourself standing before a mirror, gazing into your own eyes, and pondering, 'Am I genuinely content with where I am?' If you have, you're not alone. At the age of 54, I, too, was in that very spot. After years of balancing a demanding job and raising three incredible children as a single mother, I was confronted with that question. It wasn't just a moment of self-doubt, but a profound desire for something more—a realization that self-love isn't a luxury; it's a necessity for our happiness and well-being. I'm here to share this journey with you, understanding the complexities and challenges that accompany it.

This book is born out of that realization. It's crafted specifically for you—yes, you who might be feeling the weight of years and wondering if the best times are behind you. I'm here to guide you through a transformative journey of self-love that will deepen your relationship with yourself and enhance your interactions with others. This journey isn't just about finding happiness; it's about creating it every single day.

What sets this book apart is its practical approach. Unlike many self-help books that offer vague advice and lofty goals, I provide tangible, actionable steps. These steps are tailor-made for women over 50 who are ready to reclaim their lives. They may be small, but they are potent; they build upon each other, ensuring that you can make sustainable changes without feeling overwhelmed. This book is your tool for empowerment, equipping you to take charge of your life and prioritize your self-love and personal growth.

The journey of self-love and personal growth is a marathon, not a sprint. Each chapter of this book is carefully structured to build upon the last, allowing you to gradually incorporate new strategies into your life. You'll learn how to slowly but surely shift your mindset, habits, and, ultimately, your life's trajectory. This journey is about progress, not perfection, and I'm here to guide you every step of the way.

My journey mirrors many of yours. After leaving a high-pressure job that left me drained and disconnected, I reconnected with my spiritual side and started focusing on nurturing my inner self. This transformation took time. It required patience, resilience, and a lot of self-compassion. But the result was worth it. I am now happier and more fulfilled than ever and eager to share the lessons I've learned with you.

When you engage with this book, you're not just reading. You're arming yourself with a toolkit for life. This toolkit provides you with insights, strategies, and practical applications that bolster your journey to self-love. I encourage you to actively engage in the exercises, reflections, and journal prompts provided. Your active participation is the key to unlocking the transformative power of these pages.

Let this introduction serve as your invitation to start this vital journey. You are not alone, and it's never too late to discover your best self and lead your best life. Let's step forward into a future where self-love is the foundation for everything you do. Welcome to your new beginning. Let's get started.

CHAPTER 1

Understanding Self-Love

Do you remember the last time you complimented yourself? If you're scratching your head trying to recall, you're not alone. Many of us struggle to recognize our value, especially when dealing with the challenges of middle age. It's common to pour love and attention into our families, careers, and relationships, often leaving little in the tank for ourselves. Yet, embracing self-love is like securing your oxygen mask first in an airplane; it's essential before you can assist others effectively. This chapter is about redefining what it means to love yourself, breaking down age-old myths, and ensuring that you see self-love as a vital, life-enhancing practice perfectly tailored for the vibrant woman you are today.

1.1 DEFINING SELF-LOVE FOR THE MODERN MIDDLE-AGED WOMAN

Self-love often gets tangled in misconceptions. People frequently dismiss it as a buzzword or, worse, mistake it for narcissism. But at its core, self-love is a dynamic process of appreciating oneself that positively impacts every aspect of your life. It means showing yourself the same kindness, concern, and support you would give a good friend. When you look in the mirror, it's about greeting yourself with compassion rather than criticism. It's acknowledging that while you are not perfect, you are absolutely worthy of love and respect.

For us, as women navigating the middle chapters of our lives, self-love comes with its unique set of challenges and strengths. The physical changes, the shift in family dynamics as children grow up, and the evolution of professional roles—these transitions require us to adjust our self-perception. Self-love during this time is about giving ourselves permission to evolve and embrace these changes, recognizing the strength it takes to adapt and grow. It's also about setting boundaries that honor our time and energies—something we often overlook.

Many fear that focusing on self-love is a step towards narcissism. However, authentic self-love is the antithesis of narcissism. Narcissism involves an inflated sense of one's importance and a lack of empathy for others. In contrast, self-love encourages a healthy relationship with oneself that enhances one's capacity to care for others. It fosters respect and understanding toward ourselves, which naturally extends to those around us. By loving ourselves, we set a standard for how we want to be treated by others and decrease our tolerance for being treated poorly.

Moreover, self-love lays the foundation for personal development and fulfilling relationships. It acts as the soil from which all growth springs. When you value yourself and understand your worth, you are likelier to pursue things that nourish you and walk away from situations that deplete your spirit. Self-love empowers you to actively seek happiness and fulfillment, not just in your personal life but also in your connections with others.

Reflection Section

Take a moment to reflect on your current self-love practices. How often do you prioritize your needs and make time for self-care? Grab a journal and jot down three ways you will commit to practicing self-love this week. These could be as simple as setting aside time for a favorite hobby, saying no to an unnecessary obligation, or treating yourself to a long bath. Remember, the small steps are the ones that pave the way to real change.

Understanding and embracing self-love is the first step towards a more joyful and sustainable life. It's not just about feeling good in the moment—it's about building a life where you feel valued, respected, and whole every day.

1.2 DEBUNKING MYTHS: SELF-LOVE ISN'T SELFISHNESS

Let's tackle one of the biggest misconceptions head-on: self-love is synonymous with selfishness and vanity. It's a myth that permeates our culture, often whispered as a warning against caring too much for oneself. Yet, the reality couldn't be further from the truth. Self-love is not about neglecting your duties or stepping over others to achieve your goals. Instead, it's about nurturing yourself so that you can be more present and supportive in the lives of those you care about. Think of it this way: when you're driving a car, you need to fill up your own gas tank before you can offer a ride to someone else. Self-love operates on a similar principle—you must be in a good place before offering your best to others.

Many women, especially as they mature, find themselves playing multiple roles—caregivers, professionals, partners, mothers, and more. Each of these roles demands energy, often leaving little for oneself. In this context, self-love becomes a necessary practice to replenish this energy. It's not about vanity—it's about survival and endurance. When you practice self-love, you're not taking away from others; instead, you're ensuring you're not running on empty. This shift in perspective is crucial. It helps break down the barriers of guilt associated with self-care and reframes it as an act of kindness to oneself and those we interact with.

Furthermore, self-love leads to a more compassionate and empathetic outlook toward others. When you understand your own struggles, needs, and emotions, you become better equipped to recognize and respond to those in others. It opens up a space for empathy because you start seeing similarities rather than differences. This shift doesn't happen overnight, of course. It gradually changes as you become more attuned to your inner life. Over time, this heightened awareness can transform relationships. You might respond more patiently to a partner or be more understanding toward a coworker. That doesn't mean you become a pushover; you navigate your relationships with a clearer understanding and a firmer, yet kinder, boundary.

Self-love enables us to establish and uphold healthy boundaries. It teaches us to recognize our limits and communicate them effectively. This lesson is essential for women over 50, who often face societal pressures to always "be there" for others. Setting boundaries is a way of respecting yourself and ensuring others respect you. It's about saying, "I value my well-being, and here's what I need to maintain it." These boundaries could be like declining an additional responsibility at work when your plate is full or spending a quiet evening alone instead of attending a social gathering. These choices contribute to a healthier, more balanced life where your needs are not an afterthought.

Lastly, a strong foundation of self-love enhances our relationships with others by demonstrating how we wish to be treated. It sets a standard. When you treat yourself with kindness and respect, you naturally attract and choose to nurture relationships that reflect these values. That doesn't mean challenges vanish. However, with self-love as your guide, you navigate these challenges differently. You communicate more openly, set more explicit boundaries, and are more likely to seek solutions that respect your well-being and that of others involved. These small changes can lead to deeper, more meaningful connections with friends, family, and partners. It creates a cycle of positive interactions, where self-love amplifies the love you experience with others.

In essence, debunking the myth that self-love is selfish sets you free to explore self-love in its truest form—a form that enriches your life and the lives of everyone around you. It's about recognizing that caring deeply for oneself is one of the most selfless acts, equipping you to contribute to the world from a place of strength and abundance. With this understanding, you can move forward, knowing that each step you take towards loving yourself is a step towards a more loving, empathetic, and fulfilling life for all involved.

1.3 THE SCIENCE OF SELF-LOVE: HOW IT AFFECTS YOUR MIND AND BODY

Self-love might feel like a soft concept, wrapped in gentle affirmations and quiet moments of meditation, but its effects are grounded in hard science. A robust body of research indicates how we think about and treat ourselves can profoundly impact our mental and physical health. It's fascinating to see how a positive internal dialogue and self-care habits can change the pathways in our brains, leading to improved well-being across various aspects of our lives. Let's delve into how embracing self-love can transform your self-perception and biological health in measurable ways.

Self-love significantly reduces anxiety and depression. This connection makes intuitive sense when considering that negative self-talk and a punitive self-relationship often exacerbate these conditions. You're reprogramming your mental landscape when you shift from a critical to a supportive way of treating yourself. For instance, if you consistently remind yourself that you're capable and deserving of good things rather than berating yourself for past mistakes, you'll likely feel a lift in your mood and a decrease in anxiety-provoking thoughts. This change isn't just an emotional improvement; it's a cognitive realignment that makes resilience more accessible.

Physically, the benefits are just as compelling. Practices of self-love often include improved self-care routines such as better sleep, more nutritious eating, and regular physical activity, all of which have direct benefits for bodily health. But the influence goes deeper. Chronic stress, often a result of negative self-perception and poor mental health, has been shown to exacerbate conditions like heart disease and diabetes and can interfere with everything from gastrointestinal function to immune response. By cultivating a more compassionate self-view, you not only feel better mentally, but you also reduce the stress load on your body, helping to prevent a host of stress-related diseases. This isn't just about feeling good; it's about giving your body a chance to maintain optimal health.

Neurologically, how we think about ourselves can alter our brain structures. Engaging in self-love practices can boost the production of neurotransmitters like serotonin and dopamine, often called "feel-good hormones." This chemical shift improves mood and enhances brain plasticity—the brain's ability to change throughout life. When we practice self-affirmation, areas of the brain responsible for emotion regulation, like the prefrontal cortex, become more active. Over time, these neurological changes can lead to a more positive thinking pattern and greater mental strength, helping us to handle life's ups and downs better.

Lastly, the holistic view of health sees the mind and body as interconnected systems that complexly influence each other. Self-love strengthens this connection by improving mental health and reducing physiological stress, leading to overall well-being. It's a reciprocal relationship where improvements in mental health lead to better physical health, and improvements in physical health enhance mental well-being. For example, lowering your stress with self-love practices can boost cardiovascular health, making you feel more energetic and mentally sharp. It's all connected, and self-love is a crucial piece of the puzzle that helps to align and optimize these systems.

Understanding these scientific underpinnings can transform how we view self-love—from a nice-to-have to a must-have. It's not just about pampering yourself; it's about fundamentally improving your health and changing the structure and function of your brain. As we continue to explore the impacts of self-love, it becomes clear that starting from a place of kindness and support towards oneself isn't just a pleasant way to live; it's a powerful strategy for fostering lifelong health and stamina.

1.4 RECOGNIZING AND OVERCOMING THE INVISIBLE WOMAN SYNDROME

It's a feeling many of us know all too well, yet it rarely gets the spotlight it should—feeling invisible as we age. This phenomenon, often called the "Invisible Woman Syndrome," is not just a fleeting sense of being overlooked. It's a pervasive issue that can affect every facet of life for women entering the later chapters of their careers, their family lives, or even their social circles. It's a sense that as you grow older, your opinions, your desires, and even your presence seem to matter less to the world around you. This feeling isn't just disheartening; it can be downright eroding to one's sense of self-worth. However, the good news is this: recognition starts within, and there are powerful strategies for reclaiming the visibility and value that have always been yours.

Firstly, addressing the challenge of feeling invisible begins with acknowledging it exists. It's not just you, and it's not in your head. Society often glorifies youth, sidelining the immense value that maturity and experience bring, making it vital to start internally by recognizing your own worth independent of societal validation. Acknowledging your worth can be as simple as making a daily habit of affirming your achievements. Remind yourself of the challenges you've overcome, the projects you've led, and the people you've impacted. These affirmations are your armor against the external voices that suggest you're past your prime.

Overcoming invisibility also involves actively claiming your space and voice, especially in environments that may unwittingly overlook you. Becoming more seen could mean being more assertive during meetings or volunteering for high-visibility projects in professional settings. It's about putting your hand up, even when it feels uncomfortable, and confidently expressing your ideas. Remember, your years of experience grant you invaluable insights, and sharing these insights elevates your visibility and can drive meaningful changes in your workplace or community.

In personal and social settings, overcoming invisibility might mean initiating plans or discussions rather than waiting for an invitation. Create opportunities for engagement that play to your strengths, whether hosting a book club, leading a community project, or organizing a family gathering. Each action sends a powerful message: I am here, I matter, and I have much to contribute.

Celebrating your identity is crucial, too. Embrace and share your story, the unique journey that has shaped you into who you are today. Sharing your story could involve writing, art, or any form of expression that feels authentic to you. When you celebrate your life's narrative, you affirm your self-worth and encourage others to see and appreciate the richness of your experiences. This celebration can connect generations and cultures, cultivating a deeper understanding and appreciation for each stage of life.

As we go through these strategies, we must remember that feeling seen is not just about being noticed—it's about being understood and valued. As such, every step you take to assert your presence and voice is not just for you; it's a step towards shifting cultural perceptions and creating a more inclusive, respectful environment for all women as they age. By standing firm in your visibility, you challenge outdated stereotypes and pave the way for a society that sees age not as a decline in relevance but as an evolution of influence. So let's keep pushing forward, making our marks unapologetically, and lighting the way for future generations of women.

1.5 THE ROLE OF MINDFULNESS IN CULTIVATING SELF-LOVE

Mindfulness might sound like a modern buzzword, but it's a practice deeply rooted in ancient wisdom that has become a beacon of calm and clarity in our bustling lives. Let's delve into what mindfulness truly means and why it's so pivotal for fostering self-love, especially as we handle the complexities of midlife and beyond. Essentially, mindfulness is about being fully present in the moment, aware of where we are and what we're doing, without being overly reactive or overwhelmed by what's happening around us. Think of it as a way of tuning in rather than tuning out.

For those of us approaching or enjoying the golden years, mindfulness is a powerful way to reconnect with ourselves. It helps peel back the layers of busyness and distractions that life piles on us, allowing us to focus on our needs and desires. This focus is important because it lays the groundwork for appreciating and caring for ourselves on a deeper level. By becoming more aware of our thoughts and feelings without judgment, we start to understand what makes us tick, what gives us joy, and what we truly need to thrive. This understanding is the first step towards loving ourselves more authentically.

Now, how can we incorporate mindfulness into our daily routines? It's simpler than you might think. Start with something as basic as mindful breathing. You can do this anywhere, anytime. Take a moment to stop and take a deep breath, focusing only on your breathing. Take note of the air you breathe into your body and slowly exhale. It's not about changing the breath but noticing it. This simple act can be a powerful pause in a hectic day, bringing you back to yourself, calming and centering you.

Another pleasing mindfulness exercise is the mindful walk. The next time you walk, perhaps in your neighborhood or a nearby park, try to notice each step. Feel your feet touching the ground, the rhythm of your stride, the sounds around you, and the temperature of the air. This practice connects you with the present moment and the physical world around you, enhancing your appreciation for the simple act of movement—a celebration of what your body can do rather than how it looks.

Mindfulness helps us manage our emotions when dealing with the stress that often comes with life's second act. By fostering an attitude of mindfulness, we develop the capacity to observe our feelings without getting swept away by them. Imagine feeling overwhelmed or anxious about a family gathering or a new project. Instead of spiraling into worry, you can use mindfulness to acknowledge these feelings, understand where they're coming from, and then decide how to address them calmly. This emotional regulation is invaluable because it stops us from reacting impulsively, allowing us to handle situations gracefully and less stressfully.

Incorporating mindfulness into your daily life doesn't mean that a dramatic change is required. It can simply be engaging in mindful eating—savoring each bite of your meal, paying attention to the texture, taste, and aroma, and appreciating the nourishment it provides. Or perhaps, begin each day with a few minutes of mindful meditation, setting a calm tone and intention for the hours ahead. Over time, these moments of mindfulness accumulate, weaving a tapestry of self-awareness and self-care that supports a deeper, more sustained love for oneself.

By embracing mindfulness, we not only enhance our own lives but also enrich the lives of those around us. When calm, centered, and self-aware, we interact with others more genuinely and compassionately. We become better listeners, more empathetic friends, and more loving family members. In its beautiful simplicity, mindfulness helps us cultivate a life where self-love and mindfulness go hand in hand, each strengthening the other. As we continue to explore and practice mindfulness, we find that it's not just an exercise for the mind but a celebration of the heart and who we are at our core.

1.6 SETTING THE STAGE: PREPARING YOUR MIND AND SPACE FOR SELF-LOVE

Embarking on a path toward self-love means more than just deciding to love yourself—it's about preparing your mind and environment to nurture this transformative process. It starts with setting intentions and extends into the very spaces in which we live, creating an atmosphere that echoes our dedication to self-care and personal growth. Let's explore some practical techniques and rituals that can help solidify your commitment to self-love, turning it into a daily practice that becomes as natural as breathing.

Mental preparation is the bedrock of any meaningful change. It involves conditioning your mind to accept and actively pursue a loving relationship with yourself. One powerful technique for this is visualization. Take a few moments each day to close your eyes and imagine a version of yourself who is deeply loved and cherished—by you. See yourself going through your daily activities with peace and confidence, handling challenges with compassion and grace towards yourself. This practice helps reinforce the mindset that you are worthy of love and makes it feel more attainable and real.

Another aspect of mental preparation is the practice of affirmations. When spoken aloud daily, these cheerful, empowering statements can transform your mindset from uncertainty to confidence. Start with affirmations like "I am worthy of love and respect" or "Each day, I treat myself with kindness and patience." These affirmations act as gentle reminders throughout your day, aligning your thoughts with your intentions of self-love. I know you've heard of affirmations before and may wonder about what kind of impact they could really have. If you make them a habit, suddenly, you will realize that you actually believe the affirmations you've been working on! More on affirmations in the next chapter.

Creating a loving space is just as crucial as the mental groundwork. Your environment can significantly influence your mood and thoughts, making it important to create spaces that inspire and uplift you. Start by decluttering your living area, a task which may seem daunting but is incredibly rewarding. A disorganized room can make your mind feel cluttered, which is counterproductive when facilitating clarity and peace. Introduce elements that bring you joy and relaxation—this might be as simple as fresh flowers, scented candles, or a cozy nook with your favorite books and a soft blanket. Each element should add to a sense of sanctuary, a place where you can retreat and recharge, enveloped by personal harmony and beauty.

Integrating self-love rituals into your daily routine can also enhance this atmosphere. These rituals could be morning meditations, evening gratitude journals, or weekly self-care nights with a warm bath and a face mask. The key is consistency; these rituals should become non-negotiable parts of your day or week, sacred times reserved for nurturing your well-being. They serve as checkpoints--moments where you can pause, reflect, and cater to your needs, reinforcing the importance of self-care.

Lastly, cultivating a long-term commitment to self-love is about recognizing that this is not a one-off project but a lifelong practice. It's about promising to keep your well-being on the priority list, regardless of life's inevitable ups and downs. This commitment might mean setting boundaries that protect your time and energy, saying no to tasks that drain you, or prioritizing activities that replenish your spirit. It also means being patient with yourself and understanding that some days will be easier than others, and that's perfectly okay. The goal is not to be perfect at self-love but to be persistent and continuously return to practices and mindsets that uplift and support you.

Through these techniques and adjustments, both mental and physical, you lay down a strong foundation for self-love that is active, thriving, and long-lasting. It shifts from an idea into a functional daily experience supporting your growth and happiness at every turn. As you move forward, let these practices be your guide and reminder that you are worthy of the same love and care you so freely give to others. Let them bring you back, again and again, to a place of peace and self-acceptance, where every day is an opportunity to treat yourself with kindness and respect.

CHAPTER 2

Building a Self-Love Mindset

I magine you're walking through a beautiful, lush garden. Every step you take is a chance to notice a different flower, each with its unique color and fragrance. But instead of enjoying these flowers, you focus only on the patches of weeds, letting them define your walk through the garden. This, in a nutshell, is what negative self-talk can do to our minds. It's like walking through the garden of our lives focused solely on the weeds, forgetting to admire the flowers. Chapter 2 of our journey is about changing that focus and nurturing the garden of your mind by transforming negative self-talk into self-compassion. Let's explore how you can shift your internal dialogue to be more loving and supportive, making your mental garden beautiful and tranquil.

2.1 TRANSFORMING NEGATIVE SELF-TALK INTO SELF-COMPASSION

Identifying Negative Self-Talk

Negative self-talk can be a tricky opponent. It's often so ingrained in our daily thoughts that we don't even recognize it. It's that little voice that says you're not good enough, the one that criticizes you for the slightest mistake, or the one that doubts your ability to face new challenges. Identifying these patterns is the essential first step toward transformation. Start by tuning into your inner dialogue, particularly during moments of stress or challenge. What are you saying to yourself? Are these thoughts supportive or demeaning? Would you say them to a friend? Often, you'll find that the words you reserve for yourself are much harsher than those you would ever use with others.

Techniques for Transformation

Once you've identified the weeds of negative self-talk, it's time to cultivate a garden of kindness within your mind. This transformation involves consciously replacing negative thoughts with compassionate ones. For instance, if you think, "I can't believe I messed that up, I'm so clumsy," pause for a moment. Replace that thought with something more compassionate, like, "It's okay to make mistakes. I can learn from this and try again." This way of thinking might feel awkward or forced at first, but it becomes more natural with practice. Another effective technique is to imagine what a compassionate friend would say to you and then try to adopt that perspective.

Role of Self-Compassion

Self-compassion is not just about being nice to yourself—it's a powerful tool for personal growth. Research has shown that self-compassion leads to greater emotional resilience, less anxiety and depression, and a better overall quality of life. It allows you to acknowledge your faults and mistakes without harsh judgment, creating a safe space for growth and learning. When you embrace self-compassion, you're not just patching over the negative with positive thoughts; you're fundamentally changing how you relate to yourself, showing yourself the same kindness and understanding you would extend to a good friend.

Practicing Regularly

Like any garden, the mind requires regular care and maintenance. Make self-compassion a daily practice. This practice could be through meditation, mindful breathing, or setting aside a few minutes each day to reflect on moments where you successfully replaced a negative thought with a compassionate one. Keep a self-compassion journal, where you write down harsh thoughts and transform them into kind ones. Over time, these practices help solidify your new mindset, making self-compassion a natural part of your mental landscape.

Interactive Element: Self-Compassion Journal Prompt

Here's a simple journaling exercise to help you cultivate a habit of self-compassion. Reflect on an event from the past week where you didn't meet your expectations. Write down the negative thoughts you experienced. Now, rewrite the scenario in your journal, but respond to your thoughts with compassion and understanding this time. How does this change your perspective on the event? Keep this practice up, and watch how your self-talk transforms, fostering a gentler, more forgiving relationship with yourself.

As we move forward, remember that transforming your negative thoughts doesn't happen overnight. Just as flowers don't bloom fully the day after you plant the seeds, the practice of self-compassion takes time to cultivate. But with each small act of kindness towards yourself, you're planting seeds of change that will eventually flourish into a beautiful, thriving garden. Keep tending to it, and soon, you'll find that your walk through the garden of life is much more joyous, where you can see and appreciate the vibrant flowers among the weeds.

2.2 THE POWER OF AFFIRMATIONS: CRAFTING YOUR PERSONAL MANTRAS

Affirmations, simple yet powerful statements, can significantly alter how you think, transforming a barren field into thriving grounds. Consider affirmations as your green thumb, planting seeds of positivity and self-love that, with care and repetition, blossom into beautiful realities in your mind and life. The process of creating these affirmations should be deeply personal and resonate with your specific desires and needs. Start by identifying areas in your life where you seek change or reinforcement. Perhaps you want to cultivate more self-confidence, embrace your age with pride, or acknowledge your worth regularly. Once you pinpoint these areas, develop affirmations that speak directly to them. For instance, if self-confidence in your professional abilities is what you're nurturing, an affirmation like "I am competent, skilled, and bring valuable ideas to the table" can be your mantra. Make your affirmations specific, positive, and in the present tense, as if they are already your reality. This helps your mind accept them as truths, slowly rewriting any narratives of doubt or negativity.

Integrating affirmations into your daily routine can elevate them from mere words to profound beliefs. One practical way to do this is to kickstart your day with your affirmations. As part of your morning ritual, whether sipping your coffee or preparing for the day, repeat your affirmations aloud three times each. The act of hearing your voice affirm these positive statements helps to cement them in your mind. Another strategy is to place sticky notes with your affirmations in areas you frequent—the bathroom mirror, the refrigerator door, or next to your computer screen. Each time you encounter them, take a moment, read them, and take a deep breath, allowing the words to permeate your being. For tech-savvy people, setting reminders on your phone that display different affirmations throughout the day can be a powerful way to keep them at the forefront of your thoughts.

Of course, the shift towards building a habit of positive affirmations has its challenges. Skepticism often creeps in, especially in the beginning. You might question whether simply saying these things can make any real difference. This doubt is natural, but it's also manageable. First, understand that affirmations are not magic—they don't change your reality overnight. Instead, they work gradually to shift your mindset, influencing how you perceive and react to the world around you. This shift can lead to tangible changes in your behavior and circumstances. If skepticism persists, experiment with affirmations scientifically—commit to a set period, say three weeks, where you diligently practice your affirmations. Observe any changes in your mood, attitudes, or even your external situation. More often than not, you'll notice a shift, however subtle it may be.

Focusing affirmations on self-love is particularly transformative. As middle-aged women, society often subtly suggests that our value diminishes with age. Counter this narrative with affirmations celebrating your wisdom, experience, and continued potential. Phrases like "I grow more radiant and wise with each passing year" or "I lovingly accept myself as I am and am excited about who I am becoming" can be powerful tools in your self-love arsenal. These affirmations reinforce the idea that your age is an asset, not a liability and that your self-worth is not tied to youth but to the incredible life you've lived and continue to live. Cultivating this deep sense of self-love through affirmations enhances your well-being and models positive self-acceptance for other women in your circle, from friends to family members across generations.

In embracing affirmations, you're adjusting your thoughts and setting the stage for a life lived with intention, positivity, and deep self-respect. As these seeds of affirmation take root, you'll likely find that the landscape of your inner world becomes more vibrant, impacting your outer world in beautiful, unexpected ways.

2.3 EMBRACING VULNERABILITY AS STRENGTH

Many of us grew up thinking that to be strong, you must shield your weaknesses and always keep a composed facade. This belief, deeply ingrained in our culture, often equates vulnerability with weakness. However, what if I told you that vulnerability is a substantial strength and not a weakness? Redefining vulnerability involves understanding it not as a flaw but as a courageous step toward genuine self-expression and connection. When you allow yourself to be vulnerable, you open a window to your true self, inviting your own acceptance and deepening connections with others who see and embrace your authenticity.

Vulnerability is the cornerstone of deep, meaningful relationships. It acts as a bridge built on trust and openness, enabling us to connect more personally and profoundly. Think about a time when a friend or family member shared something personal with you that perhaps showed their fears or hopes. How did that make you feel? More often than not, such moments draw us closer, forging a stronger bond built on mutual trust and understanding. By choosing to be vulnerable, you allow others to see your true self, struggles, and triumphs, which in turn invites them to be authentic with you. This mutual exchange creates a fabric of relationships deeply rooted in truth and understanding, far from the superficial interactions that often populate our social lives.

Let me share a personal story where embracing vulnerability proved to be a strength. A few years ago, during a community meeting, I shared my struggles balancing my career and personal life. Sharing this was not easy; as someone who often took pride in maintaining a 'perfect' exterior, admitting that I was struggling felt like exposing cracks in my armor. However, the response was overwhelmingly positive. Several colleagues expressed their own similar struggles, and what followed was not only an outpouring of support but also the formation of a support group where we could share strategies and encourage one another. This experience taught me that vulnerability could lead to support, strength, and community, turning what felt like individual battles into collective journeys of growth and support.

Creating safe spaces for vulnerability is essential in fostering environments where individuals feel secure and valued. Whether in personal relationships, workplaces, or social groups, these spaces encourage open dialogue and sharing of personal experiences without fear of judgment. Start by being the change you want to see; model vulnerability by openly sharing your thoughts and feelings. Encourage others to do the same by listening actively and responding empathetically and without judgment. Establishing ground rules that promote confidentiality and respect in group settings can help facilitate a safe environment where everyone feels comfortable sharing. Remember, the goal is not to fix each other's problems but to listen and provide support to be a witness to each other's experiences.

As you continue practicing vulnerability, remember that it is not about winning or losing but courage and authenticity. It's about tearing down walls and building bridges instead. It's about replacing loneliness with connection, fear with courage, and isolation with community. Embracing vulnerability is about being open about your struggles and celebrating your joys, successes, and growth with those around you. It's about living wholeheartedly, embracing all aspects of life with open arms, and finding strength in authenticity. So next time you are hesitating to share your genuine thoughts or feelings, take a deep breath and allow yourself to be vulnerable. You might find that in your vulnerability lies your greatest strength.

2.4 LETTING GO OF PERFECTIONISM: THE ART OF BEING KIND TO YOURSELF

We've all heard that little voice in our heads that fusses over every detail, insisting that everything must be just so. It's the voice of perfectionism, and while it promises excellence, it often delivers something entirely different—stress, disappointment, and a nagging sense of never being good enough. For many of us, especially as we mature and take stock of our lives, this drive for perfection can become a heavy burden that keeps us from appreciating our real achievements and the beauty of the present moment. Understanding the pitfalls of perfectionism is crucial. It's not about lowering standards or accepting mediocrity; it's about recognizing the difference between striving for excellence and demanding the impossible from yourself.

The trap of perfectionism lies in its deception of what 'perfect' means. It tricks us into believing that we can achieve a flawless state in our looks, work, or relationships. But life, beautifully complex as it is, operates in shades of gray rather than black and white. Pursuing unattainable perfection can result in a perpetual sense of failure as goalposts keep moving. The detrimental effects are manifold—chronic stress, anxiety, and even depression can all stem from this relentless pursuit. More so, it can rob you of the ability to celebrate genuine achievements because they are never quite 'perfect.' Recognizing these traps is the first step in disarming them. It's about understanding that perfection is an illusion and that your best effort is good enough and worth celebrating.

Shifting from perfectionism to self-kindness involves a fundamental change in how you treat yourself. It's about prioritizing self-compassion over an endless chase for perfection. This shift means changing your internal dialogue to be more forgiving and less critical. For example, take a step back if you're working on a project and get caught up in minor details that aren't crucial. Remind yourself of the purpose of the project. Is the goal to be flawless, or is it to communicate an idea, solve a problem, or bring joy to someone? Refocusing on the purpose rather than the process can ease the pressure that perfectionism exerts. Practicing self-kindness also means forgiving yourself when things don't go as planned. Instead of criticizing yourself for a mistake, try acknowledging the error calmly, learning from it, and moving on. This approach reduces stress and creates more space for creativity and joy in your work.

Letting go of perfectionist tendencies isn't about a one-time fix; it's a continuous practice involving conscious daily choices. An effective strategy is to set achievable goals. Instead of a flawless presentation, aim for a clear and impactful one. Setting attainable, clear objectives helps reduce the fear of failure as the focus shifts to accomplishing defined tasks rather than chasing an elusive perfect state. Another practical step is to impose limits on your work—time limits, for instance. Allowing yourself a set amount of time to complete a task forces you to focus on what's truly important, reducing the urge to nitpick every detail. This mindset can be remarkably liberating and help increase your productivity and satisfaction.

Celebrating progress rather than perfection is a joyful and vital part of this process. Every step forward, no matter how small, is a victory worth acknowledging. Did you handle a difficult conversation with more grace than you might have in the past? Celebrate it! Did you complete a project within the deadline, even if it wasn't flawless? That's another win. Celebrating these moments reinforces the value of progress and effort over an unachievable ideal. It shifts your focus from what went wrong to what went right, building a positive feedback loop that fuels further success. This practice enhances your self-esteem and makes the journey—whatever your goal—more enjoyable and less stressful.

As you embrace kindness over perfection, you'll likely find that life becomes richer. Freed from the impossible standards of perfectionism, you can engage more fully with the world around you, savoring successes and learning from setbacks. This doesn't mean you stop striving to improve; instead, it means that improvement is a path, not a destination, and you walk with self-compassion and joy rather than harsh judgment. Remember, kindness to oneself is one of the most beautiful and powerful strokes you can paint in the art of living well.

2.5 OVERCOMING FEAR OF AGING WITH GRACE AND CONFIDENCE

Aging isn't just a biological process; it's an opportunity to experience life with a richness only time can provide. Often, society paints aging in a less-than-flattering light, focusing on the decline rather than the plethora of opportunities it brings. But here's a refreshing perspective: what if we viewed aging as a privilege? A privilege that affords us wisdom, deeper relationships, and an understanding of life that is only possible through the accumulation of unique experiences. Embracing this mindset shifts the narrative from fear to gratitude, allowing us to approach each birthday not with dread but with enthusiasm for the new possibilities each year can bring.

Building confidence as we age is integral to this shift. It involves a celebration of the self that grows bolder with time. This confidence is rooted in a deep-seated appreciation for the journey —every wrinkle, every gray hair, and every laugh line tells a story of triumph, resilience, and survival. Cultivating this confidence starts with changing how we talk to and about ourselves. It means acknowledging accomplishments, big or small, and recognizing the invaluable contributions we continue to make to our communities and families. It also means investing in ourselves— whether pursuing new educational interests, keeping physically active, or engaging in creative pursuits that ignite passion and excitement. Confidence in aging is about continuing to invest in your growth, not as a denial of aging but as an affirmation of life.

The fears associated with aging—fear of irrelevance, loss of independence, or physical decline—are natural and quite common. Confronting these fears starts with acknowledging them without judgment. Once brought into the open, you can manage these fears through proactive planning and positive thinking. For instance, maintaining physical health through regular exercise can help alleviate fears about physical decline and loss of independence. Engaging in social activities and continuing to challenge your mind can combat fears of irrelevance. Moreover, planning for the future with practical steps like health care directives, retirement planning, and discussing living arrangements can provide a sense of control that mitigates anxiety about the unknown aspects of aging.

Role models embracing aging with grace and confidence can inspire and guide us. Consider figures like Meryl Streep, who continues to dazzle on screen and stage, showing that talent and charisma do not fade with age. Or think of authors like Isabel Allende, who started a passionate career as a novelist in her forties and continues to publish thought-provoking work. These women, and countless others like them, redefine what it means to age, showing us that our later years can be equally productive, meaningful, and vibrant as our younger ones. They show us that aging is not about declining but about evolving into different versions of ourselves—versions that know more, care more, and have more to give.

Incorporating these perspectives and strategies into your life doesn't just change how you age—it transforms how you live. By viewing aging as a privilege, building confidence through continual self-investment, confronting fears with proactive strategies, and drawing inspiration from role models who thrive at every age, you set the stage for a future that's not just about growing older but growing whole—more connected to yourself, your loved ones, and the world around you. This approach doesn't just ease the fears associated with aging; it celebrates the process, turning what many dread into a journey worth embracing with enthusiasm and confidence. As you progress, let each year add to your life in number, depth, joy, and fulfillment.

2.6 CULTIVATING GRATITUDE: A DAILY PRACTICE FOR HAPPINESS

In a world that often urges us always to want more and constantly move faster, the art of gratitude offers a peaceful harbor. It's a simple yet profoundly transformative practice that enriches your life, making the ordinary extraordinary and turning everyday blessings into sources of joy and contentment. The science behind gratitude is as compelling as the practice itself; numerous studies have shown that making a habit of gratitude can significantly enhance your mental health and overall well-being. It's not just about saying thank you; it's about rewiring your brain to appreciate the present and foster an enduring sense of happiness.

Gratitude works magic by shifting your focus from what's missing in your life to what's present. It's a celebration of the now, which can dramatically decrease feelings of dissatisfaction and longing. This doesn't mean you ignore your ambitions or stop striving for better. Instead, it means you approach your goals with a mindset that appreciates what you already have rather than feeling discontented until you reach the next milestone. Such an attitude can alleviate stress and anxiety, providing a healthier, happier outlook on life. Practicing gratitude improves sleep, reduces physical ailments, and increases resilience. It creates a buffer against the negative emotions that can drain our energy and dim our outlook, making us more resilient in the face of life's inevitable challenges.

You can integrate gratitude very easily into your daily routine. One effective practice is maintaining a gratitude journal. Each night, before you sleep, write down three things you were grateful for that day. These don't have to be grand events; even small moments, like a pleasant conversation with a friend or a delicious lunch, are worth noting. This practice ends your day positively and helps you notice more things to be grateful for over time. Another method is the gratitude jar. If something good happens, write it down on paper and drop it in a jar. Watching the jar fill up can be a powerful visual reminder of all the good in your life, especially on more demanding days.

Gratitude isn't just a personal practice; it can help you tackle life's challenges more positively. When faced with a difficult situation, try to identify elements within it that you can be grateful for. For instance, if you're going through a tough time at work, you might be thankful for supportive colleagues or the opportunity to learn and grow through challenges. This strategy doesn't minimize the difficulty of the situation, but it can help you face it with a more balanced perspective, reducing feelings of overwhelm and helplessness. By focusing on what is working, you can find the strength and optimism needed to tackle what isn't.

Building a community of gratitude can amplify these benefits. Encourage everyone you know to share what they're grateful for. Start a weekly gratitude circle where everyone shares something they appreciated that week. This not only strengthens your own practice but also fosters a positive environment where appreciation and positivity thrive. It can transform relationships, enhancing empathy and understanding among group members. Seeing the world through a lens of gratitude together can create a shared language of appreciation and support, strengthening bonds and enriching everyone's experience.

As we wrap up this chapter on building a self-love mindset, remember that cultivating gratitude is more than just a practice; it's a way of life. It's about choosing to see the goodness that permeates your life, even in small, everyday moments. This choice doesn't just enhance your well-being; it radiates outward, injecting your interactions and relationships with a warmth and positivity that elevates everyone around you. As we move forward, let this spirit of gratitude guide you, enriching your journey with joy and a profound appreciation for the life you lead. As we venture into the next chapter, let's explore how this foundation of self-love and appreciation can further enhance your relationships, deepening connections and fostering a community of love and support.

CHAPTER 3

Self-Care Strategies for the Body and Soul

Remember when self-care days meant treating yourself to a spa or a long bubble bath? While those are still delightful, proper self-care encompasses much more, especially as we maneuver through our vibrant middle years and beyond. It's about creating a holistic approach that nurtures your mind, body, and soul. This chapter focuses on transforming your everyday habits into a nurturing ritual that celebrates and supports your well-being. It's about making self-care a seamless, joyful part of daily life.

3.1 NURTURING YOUR BODY: NUTRITION, EXERCISE, AND REST

Holistic Nutrition: Guidance on Nutrition that Supports Overall Well-being and Self-Love

Think of each meal as an opportunity to feed not just your body but also your spirit. Holistic nutrition focuses on consuming foods that optimize your overall health and harmonize your body's needs with your emotional well-being. This means choosing tasty and nutritious foods that fuel your body's many functions and help you combat stress, fatigue, and illness. You can incorporate your favorite fruits, vegetables, lean proteins, and whole grains into your diet. Fruits and veggies have vibrant colors representing different nutritional elements your body needs to thrive. Additionally, consider how and where you eat. Eating slowly and mindfully can transform your meal times from rushed routines into moments of peace and reflection, allowing you to fully enjoy the flavors and nourishment your food provides.

Exercise for Every Body: Promoting Inclusive, Enjoyable Forms of Physical Activity

The advantages of physical activity go far beyond weight loss. Consistent exercise is vital for maintaining strength, flexibility, and cardiovascular health, especially as we age. However, the key is finding exercise you genuinely enjoy and can keep up with in the long term. Exercise shouldn't be about pushing yourself through grueling routines that feel like punishment. It's about celebrating what your body can do, whether it's a dance class that makes you feel joyous, a yoga session that helps you find your zen, or a simple walk in the park that clears your mind and fills your lungs with fresh air. The goal is to move your body in ways that feel good and fit your lifestyle, fostering a sense of accomplishment and happiness with every step, stretch, or dance move. Nourishing your body with the proper exercise is a profound form of self-love.

The Importance of Rest: Understanding Rest as a Fundamental Aspect of Self-Care

In our non-stop world, rest often takes a back seat. It's significant to remember that rest is not laziness; it's an essential part of a healthy self-care regimen. Quality rest rejuvenates your body, helps stave off illness, sharpens your mind, and stabilizes your emotions. A nightly routine before sleeping will help your body wind down. You could turn off electric devices an hour before bed, dim the lights, and read or listen to calming music. Additionally, incorporate short breaks into your day to rest your mind—like spending a few moments with a cup of tea, doing some stretches, or just closing your eyes and breathing deeply. These little pauses can be remarkably restorative.

Integrating Self-Care: Tips for Seamlessly Incorporating Nutrition, Exercise, and Rest into Daily Life

Changing your daily routine to include these strategies can be easy. Start small and be realistic about what you can commit to daily. Consider changing one meal daily to something more nutritious, adding a ten-minute walk to your mornings, or setting a consistent bedtime. Then, build from there. Schedule these activities as you would any important appointment because they are—they're appointments with yourself, for yourself. Remember, the goal of integrating self-care isn't to add more stress to your life; it's to enrich it, making you healthier, happier, and more energized.

Interactive Element: Self-Care Planner

Consider the significant benefits of creating a weekly self-care planner. By listing your meals, planned physical activities, and designated times for rest, you not only stay organized but also receive a daily reminder to prioritize your physical health and well-being. This practical tool is an indispensable support on your journey to a fuller, more vibrant life.

As we explore self-care strategies, remember that caring for your body is not just about preventing or treating illness—it's about thriving, enjoying your life to the fullest, and honoring the incredible vehicle that carries you through this world. Guide each choice with love and respect for your body, and watch your quality of life transform.

3.2 THE IMPORTANCE OF MENTAL HEALTH DAYS

Recognizing when to take a mental health day is a skill that becomes more refined as we grow older and more attuned to our body's signals. Sometimes, the signs are evident, like feeling overwhelmed, irritable, or unusually fatigued. Other times, they're subtler, such as lacking motivation for activities you usually enjoy or snapping at loved ones over trivial matters. These indicators are your body's way of saying it needs a pause or a reset button, much like when a computer glitches after running too long without a restart. Ignoring these signals can lead to burnout. Your body is physically, emotionally, and mentally exhausted due to prolonged stress. Taking a mental health day before reaching this point can help recharge your batteries and prevent complete burnout, allowing you to return to your daily life refreshed and more capable of handling challenges.

Planning your mental health day should focus on activities that bring you inner peace and restore energy. This doesn't necessarily mean doing nothing—though, a day in bed with a good book is just the ticket for some. It might mean taking a nature walk, attending a gentle yoga class, or spending time in your garden. The key is to engage in activities that feel like a break from your routine and contribute to your well-being. This might involve creative outlets like painting or writing, which often fall by the wayside during our busy lives but are incredibly rejuvenating. Alternatively, it could involve a long-overdue catch-up with a friend who makes you laugh or a solo movie date where you lose yourself in a story. No matter what activities you choose, the goal is to make your mental health day an actual break from your everyday stresses, filled with things that replenish your spirit rather than deplete it.

Overcoming the guilt associated with taking time for yourself is a common hurdle. An inner critic often whispers you're selfish or lazy, especially if you're used to prioritizing everyone else's needs first. It's essential to silence this critic and shift your perspective to view mental health days as a necessity, not a luxury. Taking this time is not just about self-indulgence—it's about self-preservation. It helps you maintain your health and continue being there for the people you care about. Remind yourself that being at your best mentally and emotionally benefits you and everyone around you. Moreover, taking mental health days can set a positive example for others struggling to allow themselves the same care. By prioritizing your mental health openly, you encourage others to acknowledge and nurture their needs.

Mental health should always be a priority, not an afterthought. It's as essential as physical health and deserves the same care and attention. Integrating mental health days into your life is a crucial aspect of self-care that helps maintain your long-term health and happiness. Viewing these days as a preventive measure rather than a last resort can change your entire approach to mental health. It becomes about maintaining wellness rather than only responding to crises, a subtle but profound shift in how we view and handle our mental well-being. This proactive approach enhances your quality of life and ensures you are ready to handle the stresses that come your way with grace and resilience. Restoring your mental and emotional equilibrium is a wise investment in your overall health, which pays dividends in all areas of your life.

3.3 SPIRITUAL PRACTICES FOR INNER PEACE

When we talk about self-care, it's easy to focus on the tangible—things you can do with your body or choices about your diet and exercise. But a deeper layer to self-care sometimes gets overlooked: your spiritual well-being. Spirituality, often mixed with religiosity, is about connecting to something greater than yourself, which can significantly enhance your sense of peace and personal well-being. It's about finding meaning and a sense of connection, which are vital as we navigate the complexities of life in our later years.

Inviting spirituality into your life doesn't necessarily mean adhering to religious practices—unless that resonates with you. Spirituality is broader and can be as unique as each individual. It's about finding what lifts your spirit and connects you to the universe, nature, humanity, or even your deeper self. For some, this could mean meditation or yoga; both can reduce stress, improve mental clarity, and promote overall well-being. These practices can provide a quiet space in your day, allowing you to pause, breathe, and realign with your core values and desires.

For others, spirituality might involve spending time in nature, which can be incredibly grounding and healing. Whether walking through a forest, gardening, or simply sitting by the ocean, being in nature can evoke a deeply spiritual feeling of wonderment. It reminds us of our small place within the larger tapestry of life and can help put our worries and stresses into perspective. This connection to the natural world can be a powerful source of peace and renewal, especially in times of turmoil or change.

Another beautiful aspect of spirituality is the community it can create. Participating in group activities that have a spiritual component—like community gardens, choir singing, or volunteer groups—can connect you with others who share your values and enhance your sense of belonging and purpose. These connections can be uplifting and provide social and spiritual support, which is essential as we grow older.

Incorporating these spiritual routines into your daily life doesn't have to be overwhelming. You can set aside a few minutes each morning to meditate, journal, or read something that inspires you. Or perhaps it means making a weekly date with yourself to spend time in a local park or by the water. The key is consistency and intentionality—making a regular appointment with yourself to engage in these practices, knowing that they nourish your soul just as much as any meal nourishes your body.

Spirituality, in its essence, is about connection and meaning. It provides a lens through which to view your experiences, both good and bad, as part of a larger narrative. This perspective can be incredibly liberating and comforting, especially in challenging times. It offers a way to see beyond the immediate to the broader tapestry of life, finding peace in knowing that everything is interconnected and every experience holds value. Whether you find this connection in quiet contemplation, in the beauty of nature, or in the joy of community, spirituality can be a profound source of comfort, inspiration, and peace as you navigate the remarkable complexity of your life.

3.4 CREATIVE OUTLETS FOR EMOTIONAL EXPRESSION

Creativity isn't just for artists, musicians, or writers; it's a therapeutic tool available to everyone, including you, regardless of your perceived skill level. Engaging in creative activities offers a unique form of therapy that can soothe, heal, and express emotions that words alone cannot. Whether painting, gardening, writing, or even cooking, creativity offers an outlet for your feelings and can lead to substantial emotional and psychological relief. When you create, you engage parts of your brain involved in problem-solving and emotional processing, helping to alleviate stress. Think of it as decluttering your inner world by making something external. This process can be incredibly freeing, allowing you to set aside the analytical, often critical part of your brain and connect with your intuitive, emotional side. It's not about the end product but the process—the act of creation, which can be an enriching and insightful experience.

Discovering or rediscovering your creative outlet as an older adult can be thrilling. Perhaps you've always wanted to paint but never thought you had the talent, or maybe you used to write poetry before life got too busy. Now is the perfect time to explore these interests without the pressure of deadlines or expectations. Start small; for instance, join a beginner's art class or set up a small garden. The key is to find joy in the activity, regardless of the outcome. Let go of any self-judgment about being good or bad at the activity and focus more on how it makes you feel. Does it bring you peace? Excitement? A sense of accomplishment? These feelings show you're nurturing your creative side and boosting your emotional well-being.

Using creativity as a tool for emotional processing and release can be particularly powerful. Creative expression allows you to express feelings that are otherwise difficult to articulate verbally.

For example, creating something can be part of your healing process when dealing with grief or loss. You could paint using colors that evoke different aspects of your feelings or write a story that parallels your emotional journey. This doesn't mean every creative session needs to be about processing deep emotions; sometimes, just focusing on a simple creative task can be enough to give you a break from heavy feelings and bring a sense of calm and focus.

The community aspect of creativity often goes overlooked, but it is incredibly enriching. Joining a group—a knitting circle, a painting class, or a gardening club—can provide support, inspiration, and a sense of belonging and connection. These communities can become spaces where you feel safe to share ideas and emotions, celebrate progress, and even commiserate over failures together. They build on the common ground of creative endeavor, naturally fostering empathy and understanding among its members. Sharing your creative journey with others can also boost your confidence and motivation to keep exploring and expressing yourself.

As you delve into the world of creative expression, remember that the objective is not to judge your work or compare it to others but to enjoy the process and see where it takes you emotionally and spiritually. Every brushstroke, every word, every clipped branch is a step towards understanding more about yourself and finding new ways to express all the emotions you are experiencing. In this way, creativity is not just a hobby; it's a pathway to deeper self-understanding and emotional resilience, enriching your life with every creative act you undertake.

3.5 REDEFINING BEAUTY: SELF-ACCEPTANCE IN THE MIRROR

When was the last time you looked in the mirror and genuinely smiled at what you saw—not just at your reflection, but at all the stories, struggles, and successes that your image represents? In a society where beauty standards are often narrowly defined and rigorously enforced by media images and cultural narratives, it can be challenging to maintain a positive self-image as we age. These standards, which usually glorify youth and specific body types or facial features, can significantly impact our self-esteem, making us feel as if our natural aging process is something to combat rather than celebrate. It's time to shift that narrative and start a new conversation about beauty that includes all ages, shapes, and textures and celebrates them as equally beautiful.

Challenging these entrenched beauty standards begins by questioning their validity and the power we allow them to hold over us. Why should beauty be confined to such narrow limits? Who decides what is or isn't beautiful? These questions can help you detach your self-worth from these often unattainable ideals. Instead of striving to meet external standards, focus on what makes you feel good and healthy. Whether it's a skincare routine that makes your skin glow, a physical activity that keeps your body strong, or a style that suits your personality, choose what enhances your individuality over what the magazines say. Each choice that prioritizes personal well-being and confidence over conformity to arbitrary standards is a step towards broader societal change, where people celebrate beauty in its many forms.

Self-acceptance is a practice that can transform how you see yourself and, consequently, how you interact with the world. It involves recognizing and appreciating your body for the incredible things it allows you to do rather than critiquing it for how it appears. Start this practice by changing how you engage with your reflection. Every morning, as you stand in front of the mirror, make it a habit to compliment yourself. Find one thing you genuinely admire—your eyes, your smile, or how your hair falls that day—and voice it out loud. This small, daily act can gradually rewire your perceptions, leading you to recognize and celebrate your unique beauty more often. Additionally, try to extend the same kindness and admiration you offer to others to yourself. Just as you effortlessly find beauty in the people you are close to, regardless of their age or conformity to beauty standards, try to view yourself with the same loving lens.

Celebrating individuality is about letting your unique traits shine brightly. Embrace the features that set you apart, and consider how they tell a story about who you are. For instance, laugh lines can be a testament to years filled with joy and laughter, silver strands can shimmer as signs of seasoned wisdom, and an heirloom watch or a vintage dress can be your signature style that flaunts a timeless charm. Encourage others to share what they love about themselves, too. Sharing this can be particularly empowering in group settings, like gatherings with friends or family, where everyone can express and celebrate one another's unique features and stories. This collective celebration can reinforce a more inclusive and diverse definition of beauty.

Promoting the idea that beauty transcends age and is an inherent part of self-love is fundamental. It reframes the aging process as a natural, beautiful part of life's journey that brings its own kind of beauty—one characterized by wisdom, experience, and an evolving sense of self. To support this belief, seek out and support media and brands that portray diverse ages, body types, and ethnic backgrounds. Supporting films, shows, and publications celebrating diversity in beauty helps broaden the cultural understanding of beauty, making room for more stories and images that reflect the true diversity of society. This support can help change public perceptions and boost collective self-esteem, fostering a culture where everyone can feel beautiful, valued, and seen, regardless of age.

As you continue redefining beauty for yourself, remember that every step you take elevates your self-esteem and paves the way for a more inclusive, compassionate world where beauty is celebrated in all its forms. Embrace your reflection, celebrate your uniqueness, and carry forward the message that beauty is not just skin deep—it's a reflection of a life fully lived, a story continuously unfolding, and a love that grows deeper every year.

3.6 EMBRACING SEXUALITY AND INTIMACY AFTER 50

Let's talk about a topic that often gets whispered about but seldom addressed openly—sexuality and intimacy as we age. There's a common misconception that interest in sexual activity inevitably declines with age or that intimacy becomes less important. However, these beliefs are misleading and detrimental, as they can lead to feelings of being 'past one's prime.' The truth is that sexuality and the desire for intimacy are natural, ongoing aspects of our human experience, irrespective of age. Embracing this can lead to a richer, more fulfilling life and is a profound expression of self-love.

Myths surrounding sexuality in later life can create unnecessary barriers. Declining sexual desire and function due to aging is one such myth. While it's true that physiological changes can affect sexual health, these changes do not equate to a loss of sexuality or the inability to enjoy intimate moments. Many find that with age comes a deeper understanding of their body and desires, leading to a more satisfying sexual experience. It's essential to approach these changes with openness and acceptance, seeking information and possibly medical advice to manage them effectively rather than accepting them as an end to sexual enjoyment.

Promoting intimacy with oneself and your partner is vital at any stage of life, but it can take on new dimensions after 50. This might involve redefining what intimacy looks like for you. Beyond physical intimacy, emotional and intellectual connections can also provide profound satisfaction and joy. Communicating openly with your partner about your changing needs, desires, and concerns is essential. For singles, exploring new relationships can be equally rewarding. Remember, intimacy is not solely about sexual activities; it's about closeness, affection, and shared experiences. It's about feeling connected and valued, physically and emotionally.

Overcoming barriers to a fulfilling sex life often involves tackling both physical and psychological challenges. Physically, staying active and maintaining a healthy lifestyle can significantly and positively impact sexual health. This regime includes regular exercise, a nutritious diet, and adequate sleep—all of which can enhance energy levels and improve physical function. On the psychological side, addressing any emotional issues or past traumas with a therapist can be beneficial. Additionally, exploring new ways to experience intimacy, such as through massage or other forms of physical touch, can open new avenues for connection and pleasure.

Linking self-love with sexuality is perhaps the most empowering aspect of embracing your sexual self after 50. Recognize that loving yourself includes respecting and attending to your sexual needs. Self-love in this context means accepting your body as it is now, treating it with care, and allowing yourself to experience pleasure without guilt or shame. It's about affirming that you deserve love and intimacy, regardless of age. This affirmation can reinforce your self-esteem and contribute to overall well-being, making you feel more connected to your body and emotional needs.

As this chapter closes, remember that embracing your sexuality and intimacy as you age is not just about maintaining physical relationships. It's about continuing to grow in self-understanding and self-appreciation, recognizing the evolving needs and desires of each new season of life. Staying connected to yourself and others is necessary, enriching your life with joy, satisfaction, and love. Let this understanding carry you confidently forward as you continue exploring the many dimensions of self-care and self-love in the coming chapters.

CHAPTER 4

Overcoming Everyday Obstacles

With its beautiful array of experiences, life also brings many challenges that sometimes feel like obstacles in our path. Whether balancing family demands with personal time, navigating career shifts, or managing our health, each day can seem like a delicate dance of choices and compromises. For us, particularly in the rich and complex middle years of our lives, these challenges often revolve around integrating our newfound understanding of self-love with the roles we've played for decades. In this chapter, we'll explore practical strategies not just to face these challenges but to weave them into the fabric of our lives in a way that strengthens rather than diminishes our commitment to self-love. Let's begin by delving into one of the most common areas where many of us feel stretched thin—balancing self-love with family obligations.

4.1 BALANCING SELF-LOVE WITH FAMILY OBLIGATIONS

Prioritizing Self-Care: Emphasizing the Importance of Self-Care Even When Family Obligations Demand Your Attention

It's a typical Tuesday evening. You're just back from work, your phone is ringing with a call from your teenage son needing help with his homework, you need to cook dinner, and all you want is a moment to catch your breath. Sound familiar? In these moments, prioritizing self-care isn't just important—it's essential. Remember, caring for yourself is not a luxury; the fuel keeps you running. Without it, everything else starts to fall apart. By prioritizing your own well-being, you enable yourself to thrive and provide better support to those around you. Start by identifying small pockets of time dedicated solely to your self-care. It could be a 15-minute morning meditation before the house wakes up or a quick walk after dinner. These small acts of self-care can significantly boost your energy and mood, enabling you to handle family obligations with more grace and less stress.

Setting Boundaries: Strategies for Setting Healthy Boundaries with Family Members to Ensure Personal Time for Self-Love Practices

Setting boundaries is often one of the most challenging tasks, especially with family. There's a guilt associated with saying no or carving out time for oneself, particularly for women, who are often seen as perennial caregivers. It is vital to set boundaries to maintain your health and happiness. Start by clearly communicating your needs to your family. Explain why these boundaries are necessary for your well-being and the entire family's well-being. For instance, you might set a boundary that you will have an hour to yourself after dinner or that Wednesday evenings are your yoga nights. Be consistent and firm about these boundaries, but also be prepared for some pushback. It might take time for your family to adjust, but stay firm. They'll learn to respect your space and might even follow your lead in setting their own boundaries.

Communicating Needs: Tips for Effectively Communicating Your Self-Care Needs to Your Family

Effective communication ensures your family understands and respects your self-care needs. Use "I" statements to express how vital these moments are for you. For example, say, "I need thirty minutes to unwind alone in the evenings. It helps me recharge and be more present with you all afterward." Avoid using accusatory or defensive language that could lead to misunderstandings and conflict. Communicate feelings and needs clearly and calmly. It's also helpful to involve your family in self-care routines where possible. Including them helps them understand the importance of these practices and shows them how to care for their well-being.

Integration of Self-Love: Ideas for Integrating Self-Love Practices into Family Activities to Foster a Nurturing Environment for Everyone

Integrating self-love into family life can transform the home environment into a nurturing space for everyone. It can be as simple as starting a family gratitude jar, where each member shares something they're grateful for daily, or setting aside time each week for a family activity everyone enjoys. You could also introduce family meditation sessions or encourage members to share something they love about themselves during dinner. These practices foster a loving and supportive environment and teach your family the importance of self-love and care.

Interactive Element: Family Self-Care Plan

To put these strategies into action:

1. Consider creating a Family Self-Care Plan.
2. Sit down with your family and discuss ways each member can incorporate self-care into their daily routines.
3. Create a chart that includes each person's self-care activities for the week.

Charting ensures everyone's self-care needs are met and turns self-love into a shared family value. This plan can be an excellent way to unite the family, strengthen emotional bonds, and address everyone's mental and emotional needs.

Amidst the intricacies of our daily lives, remember that integrating self-love is not about achieving perfect balance or making drastic changes overnight. It's about making small, regular choices that respect our well-being and enhance our capacity to confront life's challenges with resilience and grace. Let these strategies guide you in infusing self-love into the essence of your family life, creating a harmonious equilibrium that nurtures everyone involved.

4.2 HANDLING CAREER TRANSITIONS WITH SELF-COMPASSION

When the winds of change blow through our professional lives, it's easy to feel unmoored, as if our ship has been set adrift. Whether stepping into a new role, handling a company restructuring, or even facing a job loss, career transitions are pivotal moments that can shape your resume and your personal growth and self-discovery. Embracing these changes with a positive outlook transforms them from daunting upheavals into opportunities to blossom and find new paths that align even more closely with our true passions and capabilities.

Viewing each career transition as a fresh start and a chance to expand your horizons is important. This perspective encourages strength and adaptability—qualities invaluable in professional settings and all areas of life. Instead of viewing a career change as a disruption or a setback, try seeing it as a door opening to new possibilities. Maybe this is your chance to pursue a field you've always been passionate about, or perhaps it's an opportunity to move into a role that offers better work-life balance. Whatever the case, each change brings a chance to reassess your path and realign your career with your life goals and values.

However, navigating these transitions is not just about maintaining a brave face. It's also about treating yourself with kindness and understanding through the process. Self-compassion is your ally here, helping to cushion the emotional bumps along the way. Start by recognizing that feeling uncertain or scared is entirely normal. Allow yourself to feel these emotions without judgment. Practicing mindfulness can be beneficial during these times. Every day, allocate some time to sit and breathe while quietly observing your thoughts and emotions. This practice can help you maintain a calm center and respond to changes with thoughtfulness rather than react out of fear.

Another helpful self-compassion exercise involves writing a letter to yourself from the perspective of a good friend. What would this friend say to you about the transition you're experiencing? They would likely acknowledge your feelings, remind you of your strengths, and encourage you with compassion and understanding. This exercise can be a powerful way to shift your internal dialogue from criticism or fear to encouragement and self-support.

Reframing how you view setbacks or failures during these transitions is also crucial. In the scope of your career, not every step will be forward. Some days, it might feel like you're taking two steps back. However, each perceived setback is rich with lessons. A failed project teaches you a new way of organizing tasks, or a missed job opportunity leads you to a better role that suits your skills. These are not failures but valuable lessons and stepping stones in your more extensive career journey. Maintaining a journal where you can note and reflect on these lessons can be an excellent way to solidify this reframing process.

Networking during a career transition can also significantly open new doors and ease the transition. However, networking with love and authenticity means connecting with others to see how they can help you and discover how you can contribute to their success. Approach each networking opportunity to build genuine connections. Share your experiences openly, listen actively to others, and offer your help where you can. This approach broadens your professional network and enriches it with meaningful relationships that can encourage and support you through your career transition.

Maneuvering career transitions with self-compassion makes the process less stressful and more rewarding. It allows you to grow through change, learn from each experience, and move forward with confidence and a deeper understanding of yourself and your professional journey. As you face these transitions, let self-compassion guide you, turning each new challenge into an opportunity for growth and self-discovery. Remember, every change brings a chance to redefine and realign your career, ensuring it resonates with your values, passions, and life goals.

4.3 FINANCIAL SELF-CARE: MANAGING MONEY WITH LOVE

Managing finances can sometimes feel like walking a tightrope at great heights. It's a critical aspect of our lives that requires attention and care, especially as we grow older and our financial needs and goals evolve. Adopting a mindset of financial self-care involves more than just managing money—it's about considering your financial health an important aspect of your wellness. Consider mindful spending, which is about making purchasing decisions that reflect your values and contribute to your long-term happiness and stability. It's easy to fall into the trap of impulsive buying, especially with online shopping just a click away. However, each purchase we make is essentially an investment in our lives. Does the item bring you happiness? Does it meet a need or contribute to your goals? It might be worth reconsidering the purchase if it doesn't check any of these boxes. This approach helps keep your financial health in check and aligns your spending with your values, a beautiful form of self-respect.

Financial planning can often bring about stress, conjuring images of spreadsheets filled with figures that dictate how we should live our lives. Yet, planning your finances with kindness means approaching this task with patience and understanding towards yourself. Begin by outlining your current financial situation and future needs. This outline could involve planning for retirement, setting aside funds for health care, or even preparing for leisure activities that bring you happiness. Use tools and resources that simplify this process rather than complicate it. Many apps and websites offer user-friendly budgeting templates that simplify tracking income and expenses. Consider consulting with a financial advisor who resonates with your approach to money management—one who understands that financial planning is also about designing a lifestyle that brings you joy and security.

Dealing with debt is a reality for many, and it can be a significant source of stress, impacting not just financial but also mental and emotional health. Effective debt management strategies are crucial in maintaining your credit score and peace of mind. Pay off your high-interest rate debts first, as they accumulate costs faster. Don't hesitate to reach out for help if the debt feels overwhelming. Credit counselors can offer invaluable assistance, helping you consolidate debts or adjust repayment terms to be more manageable. Seeking help is a sign of strength. It's a proactive step towards regaining your financial health, and it's as important as seeing a doctor when you're physically unwell. By addressing debt with a structured plan, you reduce the economic pressure, allowing you to focus more on the aspects of life that bring you happiness and fulfillment.

Lastly, investing in self-love might not sound like a financial strategy, but it is. This includes setting aside funds for activities and needs that nourish your soul and contribute to your personal growth. It could be a course in painting, a wellness retreat, or quality products for your health and comfort. Think of these not as indulgences but as essential investments in your well-being. Allocate a part of your budget to personal development and self-care. This allowance will enhance your quality of life and reinforce the importance of treating yourself with love and respect. These investments in your well-being can lead to a happier, more fulfilled life, proving that sometimes, we measure the best financial returns in joy and contentment rather than dollars and cents.

Guiding your financial life with love and care is one of the most empowering actions you can take. It reflects a deep respect for yourself and your journey, acknowledging that financial health is vital to overall well-being. As you continue to explore and implement these strategies, remember that each step you take in managing your money thoughtfully and lovingly is a step towards a more secure and joyful life.

4.4 DIGITAL DETOX: UNPLUGGING FOR SELF-LOVE

In an age where our smartphones cling to our hands like lifelines and screens are our windows to the world, it's easy to forget how to exist without the constant pinging of notifications. You know it's time to consider a digital detox when your first-morning ritual involves scrolling through emails, and your night ends with the blue light from your screen being the last thing you see. Signs that you might need this detox include feeling anxious when away from your phone, noticing that your real-world interactions are slipping in favor of digital ones, or simply feeling overwhelmed by the sheer volume of digital information you consume daily. These indicators suggest that your digital habits might be tipping the scales away from self-love and wellness, steering towards dependency or even addiction.

Planning your digital detox doesn't have to be daunting. Start by setting clear, achievable goals. Are you looking to reduce screen time, eliminate distractions, or improve sleep? Once your objectives are clear, outline a realistic timeframe. A weekend might be a good start to see how you fare without constant connectivity, and you can gradually increase this as you grow more accustomed to unplugging. Next, identify the devices or platforms that consume most of your time or cause you the most stress—your smartphone, social media, email, or news websites. The idea is to create a plan that's not about quitting cold turkey but about reducing and managing your digital consumption in a way that aligns with your self-love goals. Notify friends and family about your detox plan so they understand your reduced availability and can support you through this process.

During your digital detox, engage in activities that help reinforce your commitment to self-love. These pursuits could be anything from diving into that book you've been meaning to read, starting a creative project like painting or writing, or simply spending more time outdoors. Yoga and meditation can also be wonderfully enriching, as they help you reconnect with your body and mind away from digital interruptions. If you crave solitude, take long walks or explore new hobbies that keep you engaged and present in the moment. The key is to fill your newly reclaimed time with pursuits that nourish you mentally, emotionally, physically, and spiritually.

Maintaining a balanced relationship with technology in your daily life can be the most challenging part of this process. Start by integrating small changes, such as turning off notifications for certain apps, setting specific 'no screen' times during the day, or even keeping your devices out of the bedroom to improve your sleep hygiene. Make these practices part of your routine, much like any other self-care habit. Over time, these minor adjustments can significantly change how you interact with technology, transforming it from a stressful situation into something that supports your well-being. Remember, the goal of a digital detox isn't to eschew technology altogether but to ensure that your use of technology is mindful and intentional, enhancing rather than detracting from your quality of life.

4.5 DEALING WITH LONELINESS AND CULTIVATING SOLITUDE

In the quiet moments of our lives, when the day's hustle winds down, we often find ourselves grappling with loneliness or cherishing the peace of solitude. It's crucial to recognize that while both experiences involve being alone, their impacts on our well-being are vastly different. Loneliness can be seen as an emotional signal that something is missing; it's often about feeling disconnected from others and can lead to sadness or isolation. On the flip side, solitude is about finding joy and peace in being alone and using that time to reconnect with yourself on a deeper level. Embracing solitude means appreciating these quiet moments as opportunities for self-reflection and growth, turning them into nourishing experiences that enhance self-love.

One of the most enriching ways to embrace solitude is engaging in activities that foster self-discovery and personal growth. Think about what brings you inner peace and joy—perhaps it's painting, where the brush stroke creates a visible manifestation of your inner world, or maybe it's gardening, feeling the earth between your fingers as you nurture life from the soil. These activities aren't just pastimes; they are profound ways of connecting with yourself, allowing you to express your feelings and thoughts without words. Journaling is another powerful tool. Writing down your thoughts and emotions clears your mind and helps you see patterns in your thinking and behavior that may require attention. These moments of solitude can become sacred rituals of self-care, where you learn more about who you are, what you value, and, ultimately, how you want to live your life.

Cultivating a loving relationship with yourself is the best strategy to combat loneliness. This means more than just enjoying your own company; it involves understanding and caring for yourself in a way that honors your needs and desires. Set aside time each day for self-reflection, listen to your needs, and respond to them as you would to a loved one. Treat yourself with kindness, forgive your mistakes, celebrate your successes, and remind yourself that you are enough, just as you are. This ongoing relationship with yourself builds a sense of internal companionship that can help mitigate feelings of loneliness because you know you always have a supportive friend in yourself.

As you nurture this beautiful relationship with yourself and embrace the enriching solitude it brings, you'll find that the moments you spend alone are not just bearable but are among the most rewarding and fulfilling parts of your life. These moments allow you to breathe deeply, understand yourself better, and grow into the person you want to be. They are the quiet pauses in the symphony of life, where you get to tune your instrument without the rush of the surrounding orchestra. Welcome these moments, cherish them, and watch as they transform your time alone and your entire life, filling it with a more profound sense of peace and contentment.

4.6 NAVIGATING HEALTH CHALLENGES WITH POSITIVITY

When health challenges appear on our doorstep, they often bring a mix of emotions—fear, frustration, uncertainty. Yet, how we respond to these challenges can profoundly influence our physical and emotional recovery. Adopting a positive mindset isn't about ignoring the reality of these situations; it's about facing them with an attitude that promotes resilience and healing. Imagine how a sunflower tilts its head towards the light, even on the cloudiest days. It's an innate mechanism called phototropism—they orient towards the sun because it's their energy source and growth. Similarly, orienting your mind towards positive thoughts during health challenges can give you the energy and perspective needed to persevere through them.

One effective way to encourage this mindset is by practicing gratitude. Even amid health issues, there are small blessings around us—maybe it's the support from loved ones, a comfortable home, or simply a sunny day. Focusing on these positives doesn't negate your challenges but provides a more balanced perspective that can ease anxiety and foster hope. Additionally, daily gentle, positive affirmations can reinforce your mental stability. Phrases like "I am capable of getting through this" or "Each day brings opportunities for healing" serve as gentle reminders that you are more than your current situation. These affirmations can act as beacons of light, guiding you through darker times.

Integrating self-love into your treatment plans and health routines can significantly affect your journey toward recovery or management of your health conditions. This integration starts with listening to your body and respecting its limits. It means not pushing yourself too hard and treating yourself with kindness, much like treating someone you care deeply about. It also involves making informed decisions about your treatment options and being actively engaged in discussions with your healthcare providers. Educate yourself about your condition and treatment possibilities, and consider therapies that align with your values and lifestyle. Whether incorporating holistic practices like yoga and meditation or sticking to a medication regimen, choose paths that honor your body's needs and your emotional comfort.

At the heart of effectively dealing with health challenges is a solid support system. Whether composed of family, friends, or support groups, this network can offer emotional comfort and practical help. Don't hesitate to lean on these relationships. Sometimes, sharing your fears and frustrations can significantly lighten your emotional load. If you struggle to ask for help, remember that allowing others to support you can also be a gift to them. People close to you often want to help but might need to learn how or if they should offer. Communicating your needs clearly can open the door for them to provide the support you require, creating a give-and-take that strengthens bonds.

Celebrating small victories is crucial in the health journey. Every step forward, no matter how small, is a testament to your strength and tenacity. Did you walk a little farther today? Celebrate that. Did you get through a day of treatment with a smile? That's a victory. These celebrations can significantly boost your morale and are reminders of your progress, no matter the pace. They serve as milestones that mark your journey, growth, and perseverance. Acknowledge and share these achievements with your support network; let them celebrate with you and remind you how far you've come.

Handling health challenges with a positive outlook, self-love in your treatment choices, strong support systems, and a spirit of celebration turn the path of recovery into one of empowerment and personal growth. Each step taken with positivity and care contributes to your physical health and a deeper, more compassionate relationship with yourself. As we wrap up this chapter, remember that health challenges, while daunting, also bring opportunities for profound self-discovery and connection. They remind us of our durability, capacity for change, and the incredible support surrounding us. As you progress, let these insights guide you, turning challenges into opportunities to become a more complete and self-aware person. Let's carry this strength and insight into the next chapter, where we will explore developing profound relationships built on the foundation of self-love.

Make a Difference with Your Review

UNLOCK THE POWER OF GENEROSITY

Helping one person might not change the whole world, but it could change the world for one person.

— UNKNOWN

People who give without expecting anything in return live longer, happier lives. So, if we have a chance to do that during our time together, let's try it.

To make that happen, I have a question for you...

Would you help someone you've never met, even if you never got credit for it?

Who is this person, you ask? They are like you. Or, at least, like you used to be. Less experienced, wanting to make a difference, and needing help but still figuring out where to look.

Our mission is to make self-love and personal growth accessible to everyone. Everything I do stems from that mission, and the only way for me to accomplish it is by reaching...well...everyone.

This is where you come in. Most people do, in fact, judge a book by its cover (and its reviews). So here's my ask on behalf of someone just like you:

Please help that person by leaving this book a review.

Your gift costs no money and less than 60 seconds to make real, but it can change a fellow reader's life forever. Your review could help...

...one more person find their path to self-love.
...one more reader feel empowered.
...one more person believe in their ability to change.
..one more soul discover inner peace.
...one more dream come true.

To get that 'feel good' feeling and help this person for real, all you have to do is...and it takes less than 60 seconds...

Leave a review.

Simply scan the QR code to leave your review:

If you feel good about helping someone you'll never meet, you are my kind of person. Welcome to the club. You're one of us.

I'm even more excited to help you transform your life through self-love and personal growth. You'll love the practical steps and heartfelt guidance in the coming chapters.

Thank you from the bottom of my heart. Now, back to our regularly scheduled programming.

- Your biggest fan, Jillian Beanne

PS - Fun fact: If you provide something of value to another person, it makes you more valuable to them. If you'd like to spread goodwill straight from one reader to another - and you believe this book will help them - send this book their way.

CHAPTER 5

Healing from the Past

I magine you're sorting through an old box of photographs. Each picture is a snapshot of different chapters of your life, some joyous and others perhaps a little more complicated. It's not just the happy moments that shape who we are but also those tough times that we sometimes try to bury deep within the box. Healing from the past isn't about removing these pictures from our collection; it's about coming to terms with them, understanding their context, and, sometimes, placing them in a new frame where they can be viewed not with pain but with acceptance and growth. This chapter dedicates itself to gently guiding you through these snapshots, offering understanding and tools to help you heal from past traumas and rebuild a foundation of self-love that is stronger than ever.

5.1 IDENTIFYING AND HEALING FROM PAST TRAUMAS

Recognizing Trauma

Trauma can be elusive, often disguising itself amid the normality of daily life. It might show up as an irrational fear, an unexplained bout of anxiety, or an inability to trust others. Recognizing that these reactions might be rooted in past traumas is a significant first step toward healing. Trauma isn't always related to one monumental event; it can also stem from smaller, continuous stresses accumulating over time. It's essential to acknowledge that trauma can look different for everyone—it doesn't discriminate by age, and its impacts can resurface at any stage in life, especially as we grow older and perhaps more reflective.

To start recognizing signs of unresolved trauma, pay attention to emotional and physical cues. Do certain situations make you unusually nervous? Do specific types of people or relationships consistently lead to discomfort or distress? These reactions can be clues pointing to unresolved issues. It's also helpful to reflect on your life's timeline, identifying periods when you felt overwhelmed or helpless. Writing these down can provide a clearer picture and is often therapeutic.

Healing Practices

Once you've begun recognizing the areas where past trauma might affect your present, the next step is healing. This journey is deeply personal and can involve various practices, depending on what resonates with you. Mindfulness meditation is particularly effective--you must sit quietly while observing your breath, thoughts, and feelings without judgment. This meditation can help you stay centered in the here and now, providing a stable platform to process past traumas.

Creative expression is another powerful healing tool. Activities like painting, writing, or music allow you to express feelings that might be too complex or painful to articulate in words. These creative outlets provide a safe space to release emotions and can be incredibly cathartic.

Professional Support

While personal and reflective practices are invaluable, getting professional help from a therapist who specializes in trauma can be crucial. Therapists can offer guidance tailored to your specific experiences, providing strategies that are shaped by years of training and practice. They create a safe, supportive environment where you can explore your feelings and learn coping mechanisms. This professional guidance can be particularly beneficial in helping you untangle the more complex layers of your trauma.

Self-Love Post-Trauma

Rebuilding self-love after trauma is like nurturing a garden after a storm. It requires patience, care, and time. First, you need to set small, achievable goals that reinforce positive self-regard. Celebrate each accomplishment, no matter how small, and be kind to yourself through setbacks. Practicing self-compassion is critical —remember that healing is not a linear process and that having difficult days is okay.

Interactive Element: Journaling Prompt

To aid in your healing, here's a journaling prompt: Write a letter to your past self at a moment when you experienced trauma. What do you wish you could have told yourself? What support and words of kindness would have helped? This exercise can help you extend compassion to your past self and reinforce your current path of healing and self-love.

As you move forward, remember that healing from past traumas is not about erasing your history but understanding and integrating your experiences to foster a more compassionate relationship with yourself. This process allows you to take control of your story, finding strength in the knowledge that you can heal and love yourself fully, no matter your challenges.

5.2 FORGIVENESS: LETTING GO OF BITTERNESS FOR SELF-HEALING

Forgiveness is a gift you give yourself. It is the key to unlocking the chains of bitterness and resentment that may have taken root deep within your heart over the years. Often, we hold onto grudges, feeling they serve as a barrier to protecting us from getting hurt again. But these grudges weigh us down, sapping our energy and blocking our path to true peace and happiness. Embracing forgiveness allows us to shed these burdens and reclaim our emotional freedom, enhancing our capacity for self-love and opening our hearts to a more joyous existence.

The act of forgiving both ourselves and others can be transformative. Forgiveness recognizes that holding onto anger and resentment harms us more than it affects the person who wronged us. This mindset shift is not about condoning hurtful actions or dismissing your feelings. It's about acknowledging that everyone is human, capable of making mistakes and that you deserve to be free from the anger that might be poisoning your present. Begin this process by reflecting on any resentments you're harboring. Who are you angry at? What for? Have you been carrying this burden for days, months, or even years? Is it serving you, or is it time to let it go? This reflection can be uncomfortable but is also a crucial step towards healing.

Practical exercises for nurturing forgiveness in daily life can be simple and profound. One effective practice is the forgiveness letter. Compose a note to someone who you believe hurt you. Detail what they did, how it made you feel, and why it hurt you. Then, express your decision to forgive. You don't need to send this letter; its purpose is for you to articulate your feelings and make a conscious choice to forgive. Another powerful exercise is meditation focused on forgiveness. Visualize the person you want to forgive (it could even be yourself) and imagine sending them thoughts of goodwill and peace. This practice can help shift your emotional state from one of hostility to one of peace.

Releasing resentment is akin to cleaning out a closet that's been cluttered for too long. It's about making space for new emotions, experiences, and relationships. Start by acknowledging the cost of holding onto bitterness—perhaps it's keeping you from enjoying certain aspects of your life, or maybe it's affecting your relationships with others. Once you recognize these costs, actively let go of these negative feelings. This process might involve setting aside time daily to focus on the positives in your life, practicing gratitude, or using affirmations that promote forgiveness and release, such as "I choose peace over resentment." Over time, these practices can help diminish bitterness's hold on your heart.

Forgiveness ultimately leads to a sense of freedom. It liberates you from the past, allowing you to fully experience the present and embrace the future with open arms. This freedom is not just about feeling lighter or less burdened; it's about creating the emotional space that allows more joy, love, and peace into your life. As you forgive, you might find that your relationships improve, that you're more open to new experiences, and that you have a greater capacity for joy. Forgiveness doesn't mean you will forget what happened or that the memories won't still sometimes sting, but they will no longer anchor you. You will have moved on, not because what happened doesn't matter, but because you deserve to live a life filled with happiness and peace.

5.3 RELEASING GUILT: YOU'RE NOT WHAT HAPPENED TO YOU

In the tapestry of life, each thread represents a decision, an action, or an event. Some threads are vibrant, adding richness and color, while others might seem to darken the overall pattern. It's essential to remember that you are not just a single thread but the weaver of the tapestry. Your past actions or experiences, especially those that bring guilt, do not define the entirety of who you are. Separating who you are from things you've done or experienced can be liberating, allowing you to appreciate the full scope of your life's design. Understanding this separation is vital as it helps alleviate guilt that often feels suffocating.

Guilt, by its nature, ties you to a specific moment in time, continuously replaying it, often distorting it with each cycle until it becomes a colossal specter, overshadowing your self-perception. Identifying the particular instances that trigger your feelings of guilt can help you start to untangle yourself from this cycle. Is it a specific mistake, a word said in haste, or perhaps an action not taken? Once identified, approach these instances as learning opportunities rather than weights. For instance, if you feel guilty about a fallout with a friend, consider what the situation taught you about communication or empathy. Reflecting on what you've learned helps shift your focus from self-reprimand to self-improvement.

The path to overcoming guilt involves actively practicing self-compassion. This path might mean changing your internal dialogue when thoughts of guilt arise. Instead of chastising yourself, try speaking to yourself with the same kindness you would offer a dear friend in a similar situation. You might say, "Yes, I made a mistake, but that doesn't make me a bad person. I have learned from it, and I am still learning." Incorporating daily affirmations can also fortify this practice. Start your day by affirming your worth and your right to self-forgiveness, such as, "I am more than my past actions, and I forgive myself." Repeating these affirmations can gradually reshape how you view yourself, easing the burden of guilt.

Self-forgiveness is a crucial milestone on this path. It's the profound acceptance that while you cannot change the past, you can influence the present and the future. This acceptance doesn't happen overnight and often requires you to forgive yourself repeatedly. It's a process that requires you to forgive yourself each day, even multiple times a day until the weight of guilt begins to lift. Remember, self-forgiveness isn't about excusing your mistakes —it's about accepting them as part of being human and allowing yourself to move forward without self-imposed barriers.

Visual Element: Guilt Release Visualization

Imagine your guilt as a physical object—perhaps a heavy backpack you've been carrying. Visualize yourself walking towards a serene lake with this backpack. With each step, feel the weight of the guilt and how it has affected your life. When you reach the lake's edge, take a moment to acknowledge the lessons this backpack has provided, then visualize yourself taking it off and setting it down gently. See yourself walking away lighter, unburdened, free to move quickly and breathe deeply. You can return to this visualization whenever guilt starts to weigh you down again.

Guilt often masquerades as an unrelenting teacher, constantly pointing out what you did wrong without acknowledging your capacity for growth. Turning this around, viewing guilt as a teacher with valuable lessons can transform painful memories into stepping stones. What did guilt teach you about empathy, making amends, or personal limits? Each lesson is a tool that equips you better for future interactions and decisions. Documenting these lessons can be helpful; consider keeping a journal where you record instances of guilt and what each instance has taught you. This practice not only aids in processing feelings but also in recognizing patterns that might require further attention or adjustment.

As you continue to create your life, remember that each experience, whether dark or bright, adds to the overall beauty of who you are. Releasing guilt and embracing self-forgiveness allows you to continue designing with a lighter touch and a clearer vision, confident that mistakes are not just missteps but also meaningful parts of your journey.

5.4 OVERCOMING THE FEAR OF REJECTION AND FAILURE

Rejection and failure can feel like unwelcome guests knocking at our door. Perhaps you've experienced a job application that didn't pan out, a project that was not received as well as you hoped, or even a relationship that ended despite your best efforts. It's natural to feel disheartened in these moments, but there's an empowering shift that can transform these experiences from soul-crushing to life-enhancing. This shift involves reframing rejection and failure from personal defeats to redirections and opportunities for growth.

Reframing rejection starts with changing your perspective. Instead of viewing it as a personal attack or a reflection of your worth, see it as a redirection—a nudge towards a path better suited to your unique talents and journey. For instance, if a job turns you down, you might find it tempting to doubt your capabilities. However, a healthier approach is considering that you may not have been the right fit for that particular job based on your skills or life goals. That rejection is guiding you toward opportunities better aligned with your aspirations. This mindset doesn't minimize the disappointment but empowers you to maintain perspective and stay open to possibilities coming your way.

Facing and embracing the fear of failure is critical as it often holds us back from trying new things or taking risks. The fear of failing can be paralyzing, but every successful person will tell you that failure is often a pathway to success. To start embracing this fear, try visualizing the worst-case scenario and then assess how you could handle it. Usually, you'll find that even if the worst were to happen, you could still find a way forward. This exercise reduces the fear surrounding potential failures and prepares you to handle setbacks more resiliently.

Additionally, start viewing each failure as a valuable lesson. Ask yourself, what can this experience teach me? Whether it's a new insight into your work habits, a revelation about your passions, or an improvement in your skill set, each failure can refine and develop your abilities and approaches.

Establishing perseverance and self-confidence in the face of rejection and failure is like strengthening muscles—the more you work on them, the stronger they become. One effective way to build this endurance is through setting and achieving small goals. Setting realistic, achievable goals and meeting them boosts your confidence, diminishing the fear of more significant challenges. Keep these successes, no matter how small, in mind as reminders of your capabilities when doubts arise. Moreover, engage in positive self-talk. Remind yourself of your strengths and past successes regularly. This practice helps fortify your self-esteem against the impacts of future rejections or failures.

Learning from every experience of rejection and failure is vital to personal development. It's about extracting the valuable bits from disappointing experiences and using them to improve. For example, review a project critically but constructively after it fails or doesn't go as planned. Identify what went wrong and what went right. Discuss these insights with peers or mentors who can provide objective feedback and alternative strategies. This learning approach helps you improve and makes coping with setbacks easier as you start seeing them as growth opportunities rather than just losses.

When you reframe rejection, embrace the fear of failure, build stamina, and learn from each experience, you're not just turning these seemingly negative experiences into personal and professional development tools. You're undergoing a profound transformation. This proactive approach equips you to handle future challenges more effectively, enriches your understanding of your strengths and capabilities, and paves the way for a more confident and fulfilled self.

5.5 MOVING PAST THE EMPTY NEST SYNDROME

When the last child packs up their belongings and heads out to carve their own path in the world, a profound silence often settles over the home. This silence marks the beginning of what many call the empty nest syndrome, which encapsulates the myriad of emotions—sadness, loss, and sometimes confusion—that can accompany this significant life transition. While it's common to feel a sense of loss when your daily parenting duties end, it's also a pivotal moment to rediscover and reconnect with yourself in ways that might have been sidelined during the busy years of raising children.

Think of your home as an echo chamber where, for years, every corner resonated with laughter, debates, the rush of departures, and welcomes of returns. Now, the echoes have faded, and it's your turn to fill that space with sounds and pursuits that resonate with who you are beyond your role as a parent. This rediscovery is not about replacing the joy that children bring but about complementing it with personal growth and exploration. Begin by revisiting old hobbies that you might have put on hold—painting, writing, or gardening. Or, dive into new interests you've always wanted to explore but never had the time for. Enroll in that pottery class, start learning a new language, or plan that trip you've always dreamed of. Each of these steps is not just about filling time; they are acts of self-reclamation, honoring the person you are and aspire to be.

This phase can also be an excellent time to redefine your personal and professional goals. Without the constant demands of active parenting, you might have energy reserves previously tapped out. Use this newfound energy to set new career objectives, volunteer for causes you care about, or start a business venture you've pondered for years. Each goal you set and achieve during this time reinforces your capabilities and opens up new avenues of fulfillment and pride independent of your parental role.

Building and strengthening relationships in this new chapter of life is also significant. With more time at your disposal, reach out to old friends and make efforts to forge new friendships. Join clubs, groups, or classes that align with your interests. These social connections can offer support, laughter, and camaraderie, filling your life with joyful interactions and new friendships. Moreover, consider this time an opportunity to reconnect with your significant other or explore new romantic relationships. With parenting duties taking a backseat, you can rediscover each other or meet someone new who shares your current passions and dreams. These relationships can offer companionship and a chance to grow together, sharing this new phase of life with enthusiasm and mutual support.

As you journey through the empty nest syndrome, remember that feeling a mix of emotions is perfectly okay. There's no right way to adjust, but this phase has tremendous potential for personal growth and happiness. Embrace it as a period filled with opportunities— for rediscovery, new beginnings, and deepening relationships. With each step you take, you're not just moving past the empty nest syndrome but toward a more fulfilled, vibrant version of yourself, ready to enjoy this rich and rewarding chapter of your life.

5.6 FINDING CLOSURE FROM DIVORCE OR LOSS OF A PARTNER

When the partnership you thought would last forever ends, whether through divorce or losing a partner, it can feel like you've lost your footing in the world. You might find yourself enveloped in a grief that washes over you in waves, unpredictable and varying in intensity. Acknowledging this grief is the first step in your healing process. It's important to understand that grief is not just a series of emotional responses but a complex, deeply personal process that can affect every aspect of your life—your physical health, mental well-being, and interactions with others. Allow yourself to feel the full range of emotions that come with grief: the sadness, the anger, the relief, and even the fleeting moments of joy without guilt. Each emotion is a step towards healing, a sign that your heart and mind are working through the loss.

During this delicate time, prioritizing self-care is not just beneficial; it's necessary. Think of self-care as creating a nurturing environment for your wounded self. Establish routines that comfort and ground you—perhaps a nightly bath to soothe your nerves or a morning walk to connect with nature and gather your thoughts for the day. Mindful practices like meditation can also be very beneficial, helping you find a center of calm within the storm of your emotions. Moreover, nourish your body with healthy foods, engage in physical activities that boost your endorphins, and ensure you get enough rest. Remember, the mind and the body are intricately linked; caring for one aids healing the other.

Seeking support during this time can dramatically affect your healing journey. Lean on friends and family, those who understand your need for space and companionship. Don't hesitate to share your feelings with them; often, just voicing your thoughts can lighten your emotional load. Also, you can join a support group to connect with others dealing with similar losses. Hearing others' stories can provide comfort and insights you might not have considered. For some, professional help from a counselor or therapist can offer a structured path through the grieving process, equipped with tools and strategies specifically tailored to help you cope with loss and rebuild your life.

Moving forward after a significant loss involves gently looking ahead while honoring your past. Begin by setting small, manageable goals for yourself each day. These goals don't have to be monumental; they can be as simple as reading a book, visiting a friend, or attending a local event. Gradually, as you meet these goals, your confidence in your ability to face the future will grow. Start to rediscover and redefine your sense of self—who are you beyond your role as a partner? Explore new interests or revisit old hobbies that you might have set aside. This exploration is not about erasing your past but about building a future that resonates with who you are now.

As this chapter of your life gradually closes, you integrate the lessons it has taught you about love, loss, and resilience into the fabric of your being. They become part of the intricate mosaic of your life, each piece a reflection of strength and renewal. As you continue to heal, remember that it's okay to move forward at your own pace, in your way. The path ahead is open, and with each step, you rediscover the vibrancy of life, finding new ways to love, new reasons to hope, and new opportunities to connect. This chapter closes with you standing at the threshold of these new beginnings, poised to step into a future where your experiences have enriched you, making you stronger and more compassionate--now you are ready to embrace whatever comes next with an open heart and a renewed spirit.

CHAPTER 6

Cultivating Relationships with Self-Love

Have you ever agreed to something out of pressure and regretted it later? Or perhaps you've felt drained after spending time with someone who doesn't entirely respect your views or personal space. These are moments that cry out for the importance of setting boundaries. Think of boundaries in relationships like the gates in a beautiful garden; they keep what's valuable and cherished safe and secure while deciding what gets to come in and go out. This chapter is about reinforcing those gates —learning to set, communicate, and respect healthy boundaries that honor both your well-being and that of others around you.

6.1 SETTING HEALTHY BOUNDARIES IN RELATIONSHIPS

The Importance of Boundaries

Boundaries are essential for maintaining a healthy sense of self and fostering respectful, nurturing relationships. They help you define what is and what is not acceptable based on your values, limits, and needs. Without boundaries, it's easy to lose part of yourself to the demands and expectations of others, which can lead to resentment, burnout, and a loss of self-respect. More importantly, when you set clear boundaries, you allow yourself to flourish on your terms, enhancing your interactions with others. It's about knowing you have the right and responsibility to protect and honor your needs, feelings, and interests.

Identifying Your Boundary Needs

Recognizing your boundary needs starts with a deep and honest connection with your inner self. Reflect on past experiences— consider when you felt discomfort, anger, or resentment. These emotions often signal that someone has crossed a boundary. For instance, if you consistently feel exhausted after interactions with a particular friend, it might be a sign that the emotional demands of that relationship are too high, indicating a need for boundaries around your time and emotional availability. By understanding and acknowledging these feelings, you can pinpoint exactly where your limits lie, which is the first step in establishing boundaries that genuinely protect and benefit you.

Communicating Boundaries Effectively

Once you know your boundaries, the next step is communicating them clearly and confidently. This step can be daunting, especially if you need to get used to asserting yourself. Start small and straightforward. For example, if you need more space to unwind after work, you might tell your family, "I love spending time with you all, but I need 30 minutes to myself when I get home. It helps me be more present with you afterward." Remember, expressing your boundaries isn't about making demands or ultimatums; it's about sharing your needs respectfully and openly. It's also important to be consistent in enforcing these boundaries. People may forget or test limits; kindly but firmly reminding them of your boundaries helps reinforce your commitment to self-respect and healthy relationships.

Respecting Boundaries

Equally important to setting your own boundaries is respecting those established by others. This mutual respect forms a foundation of trust and safety, enabling relationships to flourish. Be mindful of verbal and non-verbal signals that indicate someone's comfort levels. It's always better to ask than assume if you need clarification. For example, before discussing a sensitive topic, ask a friend, "Is this a good time to talk about something a bit serious, or would another time be better?" This communication shows respect for their boundaries and strengthens the relational bond by demonstrating care and consideration.

Interactive Element: Boundary Reflection Exercise

Take a moment to reflect on your relationships. Think about where you might need stronger boundaries and jot these down. Next to each, write how to kindly and clearly communicate these boundaries. Practice these statements by yourself or with a trusted friend until you feel confident in expressing them naturally. This exercise prepares you to set boundaries more effectively and helps you internalize the importance of self-care and respect in all your interactions.

As you continue to navigate the complexities of relationships, remember that setting and respecting boundaries is not about building walls. Instead, it's about installing gates that allow you to control who and what affects your sanctuary of peace. Through this careful tending, you ensure that your relationships are mutually respectful, deeply caring, and wonderfully fulfilling, allowing you and those around you to grow and thrive.

6.2 COMMUNICATING YOUR NEEDS WITH CONFIDENCE

In your daily interactions, have you noticed moments when you hesitated to voice your needs? You may have stayed silent when you wanted to speak up about what you crave or require. This hesitation often stems from needing more self-awareness or the fear of appearing demanding. However, understanding and articulating your needs is not just about asserting yourself; it's about nurturing relationships where mutual respect and understanding can flourish. Start by spending some quiet time reflecting on what you truly value and need in different areas of your life, whether at work, home or in social settings. This reflection helps in crystallizing your thoughts about what matters most to you. For instance, you might realize that you need more professional acknowledgment or emotional support in your personal relationships. Identifying these needs is the first step to communicating them effectively.

Once you've identified your needs, the next step is learning to express them confidently and assertively. Assertive communication strikes a balance between aggression and passivity; it allows you to state your needs clearly and respectfully without trampling on the rights of others. This kind of communication might sound challenging if you're used to putting others' needs before your own, but it becomes more natural with practice. Begin using "I" statements that focus on your feelings rather than accusing or blaming the other person. For example, instead of saying, "You never listen to me," try, "I feel unheard when I talk about my day, and the responses are brief." This way of framing your dialogue invites a conversation rather than conflict, paving the way for a more understanding and responsive interaction.

Fear of how others will react can often deter you from expressing your needs. The fear that others might resist or reject your requests can be daunting. Addressing this fear helps one to prepare mentally before such interactions. Visualize the conversation going well, and remind yourself of your right to express your needs. It can also be helpful to start with less challenging situations to build your confidence. You'll slowly feel more capable and empowered to tackle more significant issues as you practice and see positive outcomes or constructive engagements—even if they don't always lead to the desired result.

In any relationship, whether personal or professional, understanding and accommodating the needs of others is just as fundamental as voicing your own. This two-way street enhances the quality of interactions and deepens connections. Active listening is important in this context; it involves veritably hearing what the other person is saying and showing empathy toward their needs. When someone feels genuinely heard, they are more likely to reciprocate, creating a positive, respectful, and fulfilling exchange cycle. Additionally, by being open to understanding others' needs, you often gain insights into your own, sometimes even re-evaluating what you prioritize or require in your relationships.

Learning how to effectively communicate your needs while being receptive to the needs of others transforms your interactions and relationships. It fosters an environment where everyone involved can thrive, feeling valued and understood. As you continue to practice assertive communication and active listening, you'll find that your relationships are more satisfying and less conflicted, and you will gain a stronger sense of self-respect and confidence. Maintaining this balance can be challenging, but the effort you invest in achieving it can significantly enhance your life and the lives of those around you. Remember, every conversation presents a chance to strengthen and improve your relationships.

6.3 THE ROLE OF SELF-LOVE IN ROMANTIC RELATIONSHIPS

Picture yourself standing in front of a mirror that reflects not only your appearance but your inner essence, joys, sorrows, and growth. This mirror represents self-love, a critical foundation for any romantic relationship. When you cultivate a deep appreciation and understanding of yourself, you set the stage for relationships that are not just about companionship but mutual growth and fulfillment. Self-love teaches you to value your well-being and happiness, which, in turn, attracts partners who not only admire this but are also inspired to do the same. It's akin to nurturing a garden in your soul; the better you care for it, the more it flourishes, drawing in those who appreciate its beauty.

The journey of self-love impacts how you view relationships and, importantly, the type of partners you attract. When you genuinely love and understand yourself, you naturally gravitate towards individuals who respect and encourage your personal growth. These partners are attracted to your external qualities, ability to love yourself, confidence, and approach to life. They are likely to be individuals who also invest in self-love, creating a dynamic where both partners contribute positively to each other's lives. This mutual respect and admiration form a strong foundation for a healthy, lasting relationship. It's essential to recognize that this doesn't mean a relationship without challenges but one equipped to handle them constructively.

Preserving individuality within a romantic relationship is essential, even though it can be challenging. It's easy to get swept up in the whirlwind of romance and, without realizing it, start sidelining your own needs and interests. This merging can feel exhilarating initially, but over time, it might lead to a loss of self-identity, which isn't healthy for any relationship. You must continue investing time in your hobbies, interests, and friendships outside your romantic relationship. Encourage and support your partner in doing the same. This approach maintains your individuality and keeps the relationship fresh and exciting. Each partner brings fresh thoughts, experiences, and energies into the relationship, enriching the connection. Remember, a relationship thrives best when two fully realized individuals unite and enhance each other's lives.

Handling challenges in relationships with self-love and mutual respect requires patience, empathy, and, sometimes, tough conversations. Conflict, while often viewed negatively, can be a powerful catalyst for growth and deeper understanding if handled with care. Start by recognizing that disagreements are natural. Approach them with the intent to understand rather than to win. Communicate your feelings and needs openly, and listen actively to your partner's perspective. This respectful communication fosters a safe space where both partners feel valued and heard, which is crucial for resolving conflicts in ways that strengthen the relationship.

Additionally, practice forgiving quickly and lovingly. Forgiveness doesn't mean forgetting or excusing hurtful actions; it means letting go of resentment to prevent it from damaging your relationship. This act of forgiveness, grounded in self-love and respect for each other, can transform challenges into opportunities for building a stronger partnership.

In essence, romantic relationships provide a unique reflection of how we treat ourselves and permit others to treat us.

Cultivating self-love sets a high standard for what you expect and accept from others, leading to healthier, more fulfilling relationships. As you continue to grow in self-love, you'll find that the quality of your romantic relationships grows, too, marked by a profound understanding, respect, and a genuine desire to see each other thrive. This isn't just about finding the right partner but also about being the right partner, one who loves deeply, respects fully, and grows continuously, both individually and together.

6.4 STRENGTHENING FRIENDSHIPS BY BEING YOUR AUTHENTIC SELF

In the mosaic of our lives, friendships are among the colorful threads that add color, comfort, and strength. However, the depth and quality of these relationships depend significantly on how genuinely we present ourselves. Embracing authenticity isn't just about being open about your successes and joys but also the courage to show your vulnerabilities and uncertainties. When you are your true self with friends, you invite a level of honesty that deepens your connections and creates a safe space for mutual growth and support.

One cannot overstate the importance of authenticity in friendships. It forms the foundation upon which we build trust; relationships often remain superficial without it. Think of the last time a friend opened up about a personal struggle or confessed a fear. Didn't that disclosure make you feel closer to them, perhaps even honored that they chose to share something so personal with you? When you reciprocate this openness, you nurture a friendship that's not only supportive during the highs but also resilient during the lows. Authenticity helps filter out connections not conducive to your growth, attracting and retaining those aligned with your true self.

However, being authentic, especially in new or existing social settings, can sometimes stir anxiety. The fear of judgment or rejection can be daunting, making it tempting to put up a facade. To overcome social anxiety, start with small, manageable steps. Begin by sharing your thoughts on 'safe' topics like books or movies to gauge how they're received. As you grow more comfortable, gradually share more personal opinions and experiences. Remember, every interaction doesn't need to be serious. Sometimes, simply being present and sincerely participating is enough to foster a connection. Practicing mindfulness can also be unbelievably helpful in managing anxiety. Before entering social situations, take a few moments to center yourself with some deep breaths, focusing on the present and setting intentions to engage honestly.

Trust is another critical component of deep friendships, built through consistent, honest interactions. One way to foster trust is by showing up when you say you will, whether for a casual meet-up or a moment of crisis. Additionally, being honest can strengthen trust even when it's uncomfortable. For instance, if a friend's behavior hurts you, expressing how you felt calmly and respectfully can clear the air and deepen mutual understanding and respect. It's important, however, to balance honesty with empathy—always considering how your words might affect the other person.

Choosing supportive friends plays a pivotal role in your self-love journey. Surrounding yourself with people who cheer on your successes and stand by you through your challenges is essential. A good friend sees your flaws and loves you not despite them but because of them. They encourage you without conditions and offer constructive feedback to uplift, not tear down. When looking for new friends or assessing current friendships, observe how you feel during and after interactions. Do you feel energized and valued or drained and diminished? These feelings can be indicators of whether a friendship is genuinely supportive. Also, consider how well friends respect your boundaries and accept your authentic self. Those who do are keepers.

In developing friendships that are deeply rooted in sincerity, you not only enhance your emotional and mental well-being but also create a supportive network that celebrates real connections. In these friendships, you find safe havens where you can shed masks and open hearts, where laughter flows as freely as tears, and where you meet every success and setback with understanding and encouragement. As you continue to walk the path of self-love, let your true self shine brightly, attracting people who enrich your life and inspire you to remain true to yourself in every relationship.

6.5 REBUILDING FAMILY TIES WITH COMPASSION AND PATIENCE

When it comes to family, the bonds we share are often the most enduring and, at times, the most challenging. Over the years, these bonds can become strained for various reasons, including misunderstandings, differences in values, or the pressures of everyday life. Healing and strengthening these relationships don't just improve family dynamics; they enrich our lives with a richer sense of belonging and support. The process, however, requires a gentle touch, a lot of compassion, and ample patience.

Approaching the healing of family relationships starts with a willingness to understand the perspectives of each family member involved. The healing process might mean stepping into their shoes and viewing situations through their eyes. For example, consider a long-standing disagreement with a sibling; perhaps they felt overshadowed by you during childhood, which has led to resentment. Acknowledging their feelings without immediately trying to counter them with your own can open doors to healing. It's about acknowledging their emotions and experiences, which can be a powerful catalyst for reconciliation. Remember, healing is not about who is right or wrong; it's about finding a path to mutual respect and affection. Start small—perhaps recall a shared memory that brings a smile or cook a favorite family recipe together. These small steps can slowly bridge gaps, fostering a renewed connection.

Compassionate communication is the cornerstone of rebuilding family ties. It involves speaking and listening with empathy and without judgment. This type of communication encourages open and honest dialogue, where family members feel safe to express their thoughts and feelings. For instance, if a parent feels neglected, openly discussing their feelings can help address the issue without building resentment. Using language conveying care and understanding is crucial when engaging in such conversations. Phrases like "I understand why you might feel that way" or "It wasn't my intention to make you feel unimportant" can go a long way in softening hearts and opening up channels of communication. Also, it's important to listen actively, which means fully concentrating on what is being said rather than merely waiting for your turn to speak. Listening intently demonstrates that you value the other person's feelings and viewpoints, which is fundamental in healing any relationship.

Patience is the most critical ingredient in the process of rebuilding family relationships. Healing doesn't happen overnight. It requires time and, often, multiple attempts to bridge emotional gaps. It's akin to nurturing a plant; it requires consistent care and the right environment to thrive. You might not see the fruits of your efforts immediately, but with patience, the roots of your relationship can develop deep and solid. During this time, it's vital to manage your expectations. Not all family dynamics can be ideal, and it's okay. Setting realistic expectations can prevent feelings of frustration and disappointment. For example, while you may desire a close relationship, the other person might need more space. Respecting these boundaries and adjusting your expectations can make the interactions more fulfilling and less stressful.

While rebuilding family ties, it's also essential to celebrate small victories. It could be a pleasant family dinner where everyone laughed or a heartfelt conversation that ended with a hug. These moments are significant milestones in the healing process. They reinforce the benefits of your efforts and motivate everyone involved to keep pushing forward. Remember, each positive interaction is a step toward a durable, healthier family relationship.

Trekking through the complexities of family dynamics with compassion, patience, and realistic expectations transforms not just individual relationships but the family unit as a whole. It fosters an environment of understanding and support where every member can thrive. As you apply these principles, you'll find that the ties that bind your family become more than just hardy. They become a source of security, capable of withstanding the ebbs and flows of life, enriched by deep-seated respect and love for one another. These ties are your anchor, providing reassurance and strength.

6.6 CREATING A SUPPORTIVE COMMUNITY AROUND SELF-LOVE

Finding a community that resonates with your values and supports your growth is like discovering a hidden gem in your backyard. It's there, waiting to be unearthed, providing you with support, strength, and encouragement. As we delve deeper into the theme of self-love, let's explore how you can find your tribe and foster connections that enrich your life and those around you. Think of your ideal community—the kind of people you would feel inspired and uplifted to be around. These are individuals who not only share similar interests but also embody the spirit of kindness, support, and mutual respect. To find such a tribe, start by engaging in activities that reflect your passions and values. Whether it's a book club, a gardening group, or a volunteer organization, these settings can be fertile ground for meeting people who share your interests. Attending workshops or lectures on fascinating topics can also expand your social circle. The key is to be open and proactive—sometimes, forming meaningful connections starts with a simple hello.

Once you start forming these connections, think about organizing or participating in activities that foster self-love and personal growth. For instance, you might initiate a monthly meet-up where members share something they've learned about themselves or a challenge they've overcome. This meeting deepens individual self-awareness and promotes a supportive atmosphere where members can learn from and encourage each other. Another idea could be setting up a group challenge focusing on self-care practices. Each member could set personal goals, such as meditating daily or writing gratitude lists, and the group could meet regularly to discuss progress and experiences. These activities strengthen the community bond and reinforce each member's commitment to self-love.

In today's digital age, online platforms can also be powerful in helping you find and build a supportive community. Numerous forums, social media groups, and online workshops focus on personal development and self-love themes. These platforms offer the advantage of connecting you with a diverse group of people worldwide, expanding your perspective and understanding of self-love practices. When joining online groups, look for moderated spaces to ensure respectful and constructive interactions, and don't hesitate to contribute to discussions. Sharing your journey and supporting others in their growth can be as fulfilling online as in person.

Giving back to the community can also be a profound way to enhance self-love. When you contribute to the well-being of others, you reinforce your values and the importance of kindness and support—core aspects of self-love. Think about volunteering for causes that connect with you or even start a community project that addresses a local need. Volunteering could be anything from organizing a local clean-up to starting a community garden. Not only does this provide a sense of accomplishment and connection, but it also creates a legacy of care and support within the community. Through these actions, you demonstrate that self-love is not just about how we treat ourselves but how we engage with and impact the world around us.

As you build and nurture these community ties, remember that every interaction is an opportunity to reflect the principles of self-love. You enhance your journey and contribute to a broader culture of compassion and resilience by fostering acceptance, understanding, and mutual growth. This chapter, filled with strategies and insights into forming supportive networks, aims to guide you toward a more connected and fulfilling life. As we close this chapter, let's carry forward the spirit of community and self-love, ready to explore further dimensions of personal growth in the upcoming sections. Let the relationships you develop strengthen and enrich your journey with every interaction.

CHAPTER 7
Embracing Life's Transitions

Think of the most beautiful sunrise you've ever seen. Remember how the dark, unassuming sky gradually filled with orange, pink, and gold hues, transforming the world around you. This majestic transition from night to day mirrors another profound change many face: the shift from a full-time career to retirement. It's not just a change in routine; it's a new dawn, opening up skies filled with untapped potential and unexplored adventures. As you stand on the brink of this significant life shift, let's explore how embracing this new phase can be a source of joy and renewal, not a conclusion to what was, but an exciting beginning to what's yet to come.

7.1 FROM CAREER WOMAN TO RETIREE: TRANSITIONING WITH JOY

Embracing New Beginnings

Viewing retirement as a new beginning rather than an end is critical. It's easy to feel a sense of loss as you step away from a career that has structured your days, defined part of your identity, and provided a community and purpose. However, just like the sunrise, retirement promises what's to come. It's a horizon brimming with possibilities where you can explore passions old and new without the constraints of a 9-to-5 schedule. You might have had interests squeezed into the margins of your planner or dreams deferred due to work commitments. Now, the day stretches out before you like a pristine canvas, ready to be brought to life with your dynamic colors.

Planning for Joy

Strategizing for a joyful and fulfilling retirement goes beyond financial planning, although that's undoubtedly important. It's about envisioning how you want to spend your days and who you want to spend them with. Start by listing activities that make you feel excited—travel, learning, volunteering, or perhaps starting a small business. Consider how you can structure your days to bring a sense of accomplishment and happiness. For instance, you could dedicate mornings to physical activity, like yoga or swimming, and afternoons to hobbies or social engagements. This restructuring doesn't have to be a rigid schedule but a flow that feels fulfilling and productive. Planning for joy might also involve learning new technologies or tools to help you stay connected with friends and family, pursue new hobbies, or manage your health and home more efficiently.

Identity Beyond Work

One of the most significant shifts in retirement is the change in your professional identity. You're no longer 'the manager,' 'the teacher,' or 'the accountant.' This transition can feel unsettling, but it also opens up an opportunity to redefine who you are and how you see yourself. You might rediscover aspects of your personality overshadowed by your professional role or find new traits you still need to explore. Delve into self-reflection to uncover what holds the most value for you now. What values do you hold dear? What legacy do you wish to leave behind? The timing could be perfect to write that book, mentor younger professionals in your field, or become an activist for a cause you're passionate about. Your work identity was just one chapter in your life; retirement turns the page to a new chapter where you can be whoever you choose to be.

Self-Love Practices for Transition

Successfully maneuvering this transition to retirement requires nurturing your cognitive and emotional health just as you would your physical health. One way to do this is by developing self-love practices that reinforce your sense of self-worth and independence. Consider starting a transition journal to document your feelings about retirement, hopes, and challenges you face. Reflecting on these entries can provide insights and help you manage your emotions about this significant change. Equally important is the role of routines in embedding self-care into your daily life. Whether it's morning meditation, weekly lunches with friends, or simply time spent in nature, ensure these activities are non-negotiable parts of your week. They're not just activities but affirmations of your commitment to enjoying and valuing this new phase of life.

Transitioning from a full-time career to retirement is like watching a beautiful sunrise. It's the start of something new and beautiful, filled with potential and promise. As you embark on this phase, remember that it's not just about ending a career but about beginning a life enriched with freedom, joy, and self-discovery. Embrace it with open arms and a heart eager to explore new possibilities.

7.2 THE ADVENTURE OF REDISCOVERY: WHO ARE YOU POST-RETIREMENT?

Retirement often opens up a vast landscape of time and opportunity that can feel both exhilarating and daunting. Without the daily demands of a job, you might find yourself pondering, "What now?" This phase offers a perfect opportunity to rediscover and dive deep into interests you may have put on hold during your career years. Whether it's reigniting past passions or exploring new avenues that pique your curiosity, this time is your canvas, and you hold the brush. Begin by revisiting old hobbies that once brought joy and satisfaction. It could be the guitar sitting in the corner of your room gathering dust or the garden waiting for your undivided attention. Alternatively, you might find excitement in completely new pursuits. Have you ever thought about photography or perhaps learning about astronomy? The key is to follow your excitement, no matter where it leads. This exploration is not about filling time; it's about enriching your life with activities that resonate with your soul.

Creating a new routine in retirement can also bring a refreshing structure to your days. While the absence of a 9-to-5 schedule is liberating, having a flexible yet consistent routine can prevent the familiar post-retirement feeling of aimlessness. Start simple. Dedicate mornings to physical activity—a walk, a swim, or a cycle —anything that gets your body moving and heart pumping. Reserve afternoons for intellectual or creative activities like reading, crafting, or even attending workshops and classes. Evenings could be for social interactions, whether family dinners, meeting friends, or engaging in community events. This rhythm keeps you physically and mentally active and ensures you achieve holistic well-being with daily self-care, learning, and socializing.

Striking the perfect mix of personal time and communal engagement is another aspect of post-retirement that can profoundly affect your happiness. Solitude offers precious moments for reflection and self-connection, supporting you in discovering your inner self and what you desire at this stage. It's these quiet moments that often spark creativity and insight. On the other hand, too much solitude can foster loneliness. That's where the importance of community comes into play. Engaging with others through volunteer work, clubs, or local events can provide a sense of purpose and belonging. It's about creating a network of support and friendship that energizes you. You might join a book club that aligns with your love for literature or get involved in a local gardening project where you can beautify your community while meeting fellow gardening enthusiasts. The social interactions derived from these communities provide emotional nourishment and a sense of interconnectedness, which are vital for maintaining a joyful spirit.

Setting personal growth and enjoyment goals is crucial in maximizing your post-retirement years. These goals can range from the simple to the sublime. Maybe you want to master a new language or travel to a country you've always dreamed of visiting. Perhaps your goal is to write a book or to teach a class. Setting these goals gives you something exciting to work towards, injecting your days with purpose and anticipation. It's about challenging yourself to grow and expand in new directions at your own pace and on your terms. Joy and curiosity should drive these goals, not pressure or a sense of duty. They are not just tasks to tick off but experiences to enjoy, paths leading to greater fulfillment and self-discovery.

As you move through this phase of rediscovery, remember that this stage of your life offers a unique opportunity to design your days exactly how you want them. It's a chance to delve into the depths of your passions, create new routines that energize and fulfill you, balance the quiet of solitude with the joy of community, and set goals that excite and inspire you. Embrace this time with open arms and an open heart, ready to explore all the beautiful possibilities that await.

7.3 DATING AFTER 50: LOVE, SEX, AND INTIMACY

Returning to the dating scene after 50 might feel like venturing into a mysterious new world. Whether you're beginning to date again after a prolonged relationship or have decided it's time to seek companionship, it's natural to feel a mix of excitement and nerves. The key to confidently navigating this experience lies in maintaining a positive self-image and setting clear intentions about what you want. Start by updating your social skills; a coffee date, for instance, can be a low-pressure way to meet someone new. Dress to make you feel confident and comfortable, reflecting your personality. Confidence is attractive at any age, and being yourself is your greatest asset.

When re-entering the dating world, it's crucial to communicate openly and honestly. Set realistic expectations for yourself and the people you will meet. Be clear about your desires, whether seeking a long-term relationship or simply looking for friendship and companionship. Listening actively to your date's expectations and boundaries is also essential, ensuring mutual respect and understanding. This transparency will help build meaningful connections based on trust and mutual interests. Also, try different settings to meet potential partners. Group activities that align with your interests are great because they provide a natural environment for meeting people with similar passions. Whether it's a book club, dance class, or art workshop, these venues allow you to enjoy a hobby while opening the door to new romantic possibilities.

Self-love plays a pivotal role in the world of dating and relationships. By nurturing integral self-love, you set a foundation for healthy interactions and avoid settling for less than you deserve. Self-love encourages you to uphold your standards and seek a partner who respects and values you. It also helps you to rebound from setbacks or rejections with resilience, viewing them as steps along the path rather than as roadblocks. Remember, every interaction teaches you more about your preferences, boundaries, and desires. Embrace each experience as an opportunity for growth and clarification about what you seek in a relationship.

Dealing with changes in physical intimacy as we age can be another aspect of dating that might feel challenging. It's essential to embrace these changes with openness and acceptance. Communicate with your partner about any concerns or discomforts you might have, and be willing to listen to theirs as well. These exchanges can include discussions about physical limitations or changes in sexual desire that occur naturally with age. Approach these conversations with sensitivity and care, ensuring you and your partner feel respected and understood. Exploring new ways to experience intimacy can also be rewarding. Sometimes, simply holding hands, sharing a long hug, or other forms of physical closeness can enhance intimacy without pressure. The key is maintaining an open dialogue and finding mutual comfort levels, allowing intimacy to be a source of joy and connection.

Online dating has emerged as a common way to meet new people, especially when traditional settings don't always match our modern, busy lifestyles. However, maneuvering online platforms can seem daunting at first. Choose reputable dating sites that cater to older adults or align with your interests and values. Create an honest and appealing profile clearly stating what you want in a partner. Be cautious yet open-minded about online interactions. Trust your instincts—if something feels off, it probably is. Arrange your first meetings in public spaces, and consider having a friend know your whereabouts. The Internet offers an excellent way to connect with potential partners, but using it wisely and safely is imperative to protecting your privacy and well-being.

As you explore the realms of love, sex, and intimacy after 50, remember that this phase of your life holds as much potential for excitement and fulfillment as any other. With the right approach, a healthy dose of self-love, and clear communication, you can enjoy deep, meaningful connections that enrich your days and support your personal growth and happiness journey. Whether through traditional dating, online platforms, or social groups, the opportunities to meet someone special are abundant. Embrace this time with optimism and openness, ready to experience all the joys that relationships can bring at this remarkable stage of life.

7.4 GRANDPARENTING: A NEW ROLE TO LOVE

The role of a grandparent comes with a unique set of joys and responsibilities that can enrich your life in unexpected ways. The magic of this role often lies in the joyous interactions with your grandchildren, where you experience the world through their eyes, which are full of wonder and curiosity. This new chapter in your life offers the fantastic opportunity to influence and shape young lives while enjoying a connection distinct from the parental bond. Grandchildren often view their grandparents as sources of wisdom and fun, which can bring a new sense of purpose and delight to their days.

As you embrace this role, it's important to celebrate the distinct joys it brings. Grandparenting allows you to provide the kind of unconditional love and support that can be a steady presence in a child's life. You can discuss the events and moments from your life, passing on family traditions and values that help root children in their heritage. Additionally, this role often comes with the freedom to spoil them in ways parents might not—extra cookies, late bedtimes during sleepovers, or impromptu trips to the park. However, it's not just about the fun and games; it's about the deep emotional connection that can develop. These relationships can be incredibly fulfilling, providing you and your grandchildren with love and security.

Setting healthy boundaries within the family dynamic is crucial to maintaining the joy and balance of your grandparenting role. It's important to communicate openly with your children—your grandchildren's parents—about your boundaries regarding caregiving. Discuss and agree upon your roles and responsibilities to avoid misunderstandings that could lead to stress or conflict. For instance, if you're willing to babysit, clarify how often and under what circumstances you'd be available to help. Respect the parenting rules set by your children, and discuss any disagreements privately without undermining their authority in front of the grandchildren. This respect for boundaries helps maintain harmony within the family and sets a positive example for your grandchildren.

Being actively engaged in your grandchildren's lives is a fabulous way to strengthen your bond with them while fostering their independence. Take an interest in their hobbies and activities. Attend their school plays, sports games, or any extracurricular activities they're involved in. You could also engage in activities you enjoy together, such as gardening, baking, or reading stories. These shared experiences can be precious and form lasting memories. However, it's also vital to encourage their independence by supporting their efforts to try new things independently or solve problems themselves before stepping in to help. This balance of involvement and autonomy is key to fostering their growth and self-confidence while deepening their relationship with you.

Maintaining self-care practices and personal interests as a grandparent is essential for your well-being. It enables you to be fully present and engaged during the time spent with your grandchildren. It can be easy to get swept up in the joy and responsibilities of grandparenting, but remember to also take time for yourself. Keep engaging in your hobbies and interests and maintain a social life outside your family. Regular workouts, proper nutrition, and ample sleep are fundamental to keep you energized and at your best. Engaging in activities that you love and that challenge you mentally and physically can keep you spirited and help you bring more to your role as a grandparent. Keeping a journal can also be a terrific way to reflect on your experiences, celebrate the joys, and traverse the challenges of grandparenting.

Embracing the role of a grandparent can be one of the most rewarding experiences of your later years. As a grandparent, you experience unique joys, build meaningful connections, and see the world anew through the eyes of your grandchildren. Remember to enjoy every moment, set healthy boundaries, stay actively involved, and take good care of yourself, ensuring that these years are as enriching for you as they are for your grandchildren.

7.5 MOVING OR DOWNSIZING: LETTING GO AND STARTING FRESH

Moving or downsizing your living space often significantly shifts life's chapters. It might come after the kids have flown the nest, post-retirement, or simply as a choice to simplify your lifestyle. While the practical steps of sorting and packing are tangible, preparing emotionally for this change is equally important. It's not just about moving physical objects from one place to another. It involves transitioning through life phases, which can stir emotions —excitement for what's new, nostalgia, and sadness for what you're leaving behind. To navigate this emotional landscape:

1. Start by acknowledging your feelings.
2. Allow yourself a moment to sit with each emotion, whether it's joy, fear, or sorrow.
3. Recognize that it's normal to feel a sense of loss when letting go of a home filled with memories.
4. Set aside a day to review old photos and mementos, allowing yourself to reminisce and celebrate your life in your current home.

This process can be healing, transforming grief into gratitude for the experiences that have enriched your life.

As you prepare to let go of possessions, approach the process with love and mindfulness. This process isn't just about decluttering; it's a meaningful exercise in assessing what truly adds value to your life. Instead of hastily discarding items, take a moment to consider their significance. For items with special memories, consider taking photos before letting them go or repurposing them in new ways. If you find this process overwhelming, invite a caring friend or family member who can extend emotional support and practical aid. They can provide a different perspective, helping you decide what to keep, donate, or discard. Remember, letting go is not about loss—it's about making room for new experiences and joys. It's also a chance to gift items with sentimental value to friends or family who will appreciate and cherish them as much as you have.

Creating a new space that reflects your current needs and desires can be a refreshing part of moving. This is your chance to design an environment that feels like a sanctuary. Consider what elements make you feel most at home. Is it lots of natural light? A dedicated space for reading or crafts? As you set up your new home, choose options that suit your current way of life and tastes. For instance, you might opt for a more open layout that accommodates family gatherings or a smaller, cozy space that's easy to maintain and feels snug. Think about color schemes, artworks, and decorations that resonate with your sense of beauty and comfort. The goal is to create a space that meets your functional needs, uplifts your spirit, and promotes your well-being.

Engaging with a new community after a move is necessary for your emotional and social well-being. Establishing new relationships, especially later in life, can be daunting, but it allows you to expand your network and engage in novel experiences. Start by exploring local activities or clubs that align with your interests. Whether it's a gardening group, a book club, or a yoga class, these can be great places to meet people who share similar passions. Don't hesitate to introduce yourself to neighbors and participate in community events. These interactions can lead to friendships and connections that make your new environment feel like home.

Volunteering offers a fulfilling way to connect with your new community. It allows you to give back, meet people, and feel a part of something larger than yourself. As you build these new bridges, you'll find that they help you settle into your new life and enrich it with diverse interactions and new perspectives.

7.6 TAKING UP NEW HOBBIES AND PASSIONS

Visualize yourself at the edge of a boundless, inviting sea. Each wave that brushes against your feet is a new hobby or passion, inviting you to dive in and explore its depths. It's painting, pottery, or even paragliding that catches your eye. Whatever it may be, hobbies are not just activities; they're gateways to expressing and discovering unexplored facets of yourself. As we age, life offers us more time and opportunities to try new experiences and create a masterpiece that's uniquely ours.

Using hobbies to explore and express different aspects of self can be remarkably fulfilling. Each new interest provides a mirror reflecting parts of you that might have been dormant or undiscovered. For instance, painting might reveal a love for color and form, or learning to play a musical instrument might uncover a rhythmic side you never knew you had. These activities do more than fill time; they enrich your life, providing joy and a sense of achievement. They also offer therapeutic benefits, helping to alleviate stress and keep the mind active and engaged. Engaging deeply in these hobbies allows you to weave a richer tapestry of self, filled with varied interests and skills that enhance your self-image and life satisfaction.

Embracing learning new skills as an act of self-love and growth is a powerful mindset. Each time you learn something new, you say 'yes' to growth and 'no' to the stagnant waters of complacency. Learning is an affirmation of your capabilities and potential, no matter your age. It reinforces the belief that growth is a lifelong process and you can continuously evolve. This approach keeps your brain sharp and fills your heart with pride and your days with excitement. The joy of learning can be particularly profound when shared by taking a class or joining a workshop, where the communal energy of discovery and progress is palpable.

Finding community through shared interests and hobbies can significantly enhance your social life and emotional well-being. These communities provide a sense of belonging and an opportunity to connect with others on a deeper level. Whether it's a knitting circle, a book club, or a hiking group, the bonds formed over shared interests are often solid and supportive. These relationships become precious because they build on mutual respect and shared passions. They offer companionship, motivation, and inspiration as you encourage each other to improve and even compete in friendly challenges. The support network you build can become paramount to your social life, providing emotional support and camaraderie.

Overcoming fears and barriers to starting new hobbies at an older age is a common challenge. It's natural to feel hesitations—fear of failure, thoughts of being 'too old,' or worries about not fitting in. However, it's important to challenge these fears with positive affirmations and a can-do attitude. Start small if large leaps seem daunting. If you're interested in photography, start by taking photos with your phone before investing in sophisticated equipment. Join beginner classes where everyone starts from scratch, making learning new skills less intimidating. Remember, everyone was a beginner at some point, and most communities welcome newcomers. By taking these small steps, you gradually build confidence, making tackling more significant challenges easier.

As you delve into new hobbies and passions, you fill your time and expand your world. These activities bring new joys, challenges, and discoveries that enhance your life's journey. They allow you to express yourself, connect with others, and grow in beautiful and unexpected ways. So, take that first step, pick up that brush, strum that guitar, or plant that garden. Let your hobbies be the vessels that carry you through an exciting exploration of your passions and potential. Every new skill and friendship you acquire adds depth and sparkle to your life.

As this chapter closes, remember the infinite possibilities of hobbies and passions. They're pastimes and pathways to growth, joy, and fulfillment. As you turn the page, ready to explore the art of living a full and vivid life, carry the lessons and inspirations from these pursuits, allowing them to color your days and enrich your experiences, onward to more discoveries and joys in the next chapter of this exciting adventure.

CHAPTER 8

Leaving a Legacy of Love

Picture yourself on the shoreline of a placid lake, tossing a stone into the water and watching the ripples expand outward, far beyond the initial point of impact. Each ripple represents your influence through acts of kindness and giving back, touching lives and communities in unseen ways. This chapter is about transforming your actions into lasting legacies of love, beginning with one of the most heartfelt contributions you can make: volunteering.

8.1 VOLUNTEERING AND GIVING BACK: LOVE IN ACTION

Perhaps you've felt a tug at your heartstrings when hearing about needs in your community or watching stories that highlight the struggles of others. That pull you feel is not just empathy; it's also a call to action—a whisper of your potential to make a difference. Volunteering your time and talents is not just about filling hours; it's about enriching lives, including your own. Identify causes or issues that ignite your passion and find volunteering opportunities that resonate personally. Is it animal welfare, child education, or perhaps environmental conservation? Once you've pinpointed your interest areas, look for local organizations that align with those passions. Platforms like VolunteerMatch or Idealist can connect you with numerous projects that benefit from your enthusiasm and skills. Don't hesitate to reach out to these organizations and discuss how you can contribute in ways that are meaningful to you.

The impact of giving back extends beyond the immediate benefits to the community; it also profoundly influences your self-love. Each time you volunteer, you affirm your values and ability to contribute positively to the world. This affirmation builds self-esteem and a sense of purpose, which are fundamental components of self-love. Moreover, volunteering provides a sense of belonging and connection. Working alongside others who share your values fosters a community of mutual support and shared goals. It's a powerful reminder that you are not alone in your desire to improve the world. This community connection enhances your social network and deepens your sense of engagement with the world around you.

Leveraging your skills and experiences in volunteering efforts can maximize the impact of your contributions. Take a moment to inventory your skills and consider how they might benefit others. Are you a retired teacher who can tutor children? Do you have a knack for gardening that could beautify local public spaces? Or could your business career help a nonprofit streamline its operations? By aligning your skills with your volunteering efforts, you not only increase the benefit to the community but also engage in activities that are joyful and fulfilling to you. This alignment ensures that your volunteering experiences are rewarding and energizing rather than draining.

Interactive Element: Skills Inventory Exercise

Take a few minutes to list your skills and experiences that could benefit others. Next to each skill, jot down potential volunteering opportunities that could utilize this skill. For example, if you're skilled in carpentry, you might list opportunities to help build homes with a local housing charity. This exercise can help you visualize the impact of your skills and inspire you to take action.

Volunteering is a profound expression of love in action. It's about using your time, talents, and compassion to touch lives and create ripples of kindness that extend far beyond the immediate effects of your efforts. Each act of volunteering, no matter how small, has the potential to create a ripple effect, inspiring others to do the same. As you give back to the community, you'll find that the love you share comes back to you in countless ways—enhancing your feelings of self-worth, connecting you with others, and reinforcing your impact on the world. So, as you consider the legacy of love you wish to leave, remember that each act of volunteering is a powerful chapter in that legacy—a testament to your compassion and a beacon of hope in the community. As you move forward, let your actions speak loudly of your love and commitment to improving the world.

8.2 TEACHING SELF-LOVE TO THE YOUNGER GENERATION

Imagine the influence you wield merely by how you treat yourself, especially in the eyes of the younger ones around you, be it your children, grandchildren, nieces, nephews, or even the kids next door. How you navigate your self-esteem, body image, and daily self-care routines sets a blueprint for them. Being a role model of self-love isn't about perfection; it's about authenticity. It shows them that loving oneself is a natural part of life and that it's okay to feel proud of their achievements and accept their imperfections. For instance, when you openly appreciate your strengths and talk about your challenges without self-criticism, you teach them that self-love is about embracing the self, not just the 'good' parts.

Role modeling goes beyond words; it permeates everyday actions. When you choose healthy food, engage in regular physical activity, or set aside time for relaxation and hobbies, you demonstrate that self-care is a priority. These actions help instill habits that form the backbone of physical and mental health. Moreover, when they see you standing up for yourself, setting boundaries, and treating yourself with respect and kindness, you show them that self-love also involves self-respect. This can profoundly influence how they view themselves and teach them to demand respect from others, which is crucial in developing healthy relationships.

Encouraging open conversations about self-esteem, body image, and self-care is vital in fostering a safe space for them to express their thoughts and struggles. Start these discussions at a young age to build trust and openness. Discuss media influence on body image, discuss the unrealistic standards often portrayed, and share your experiences dealing with these pressures. This dialogue can help them develop a critical eye toward these influences and build a healthier, more accepting view of themselves. It's also important to listen actively to their concerns without judgment. This supportive communication validates their feelings and encourages them to share more openly, strengthening your relationship and providing them with the emotional tools to face their challenges.

Engaging in activities that boost self-love and confidence can be fun and educational. For example, participating in sports or arts improves physical and creative skills and boosts self-esteem as they achieve milestones. Activities like cooking together can also enhance self-love as they take pride in creating something others can enjoy. Moreover, engaging in self-care practices like meditation or yoga can help them cultivate mindfulness and emotional balance from a young age. These shared activities bring joy and bonding and subtly teach them the importance of self-care and self-appreciation.

Leaving a legacy of confidence and self-love for future generations is one of the most valuable gifts you can offer. It goes beyond material inheritance; it's about passing down values supporting their emotional and mental well-being throughout their lives. They build this legacy through consistent acts of self-love, open communication, and shared experiences that enrich their understanding and practice of loving themselves. By embedding these principles in their upbringing, you equip them with the tools to guide their lives with confidence, respect, and genuine self-appreciation. These lessons, deeply rooted in the experiences and memories you create together, will resonate throughout their lives, guiding them to build their happiness and spreading the message of self-love to future generations.

8.3 WRITING YOUR STORY: SHARING YOUR JOURNEY OF SELF-LOVE

There's something uniquely powerful about putting pen to paper and letting your life's stories flow. Writing your personal narrative or memoir isn't just about recording events; it's about capturing the essence of your experiences, the growth you've achieved, and the obstacles you've overcome. This act of writing can be a profound exercise in self-reflection and discovery. It allows you to see your self-love and personal development progress, sometimes revealing insights you weren't consciously aware of. If you're considering documenting your journey, start with moments that stand out—times of change, decision, or realization. These don't have to be monumental on a global scale; their significance is entirely personal to you. Reflect on what these moments taught you about loving and valuing yourself. How did they shape the person you are today? As you write, focus on the emotions and lessons rather than just the chronological details. This approach helps to convey the depth of your experiences, making your narrative richer and more engaging.

The act of writing itself offers therapeutic benefits. It can be cathartic, helping clear emotional blockages and offering relief. As you articulate your struggles and victories, you might find a new perspective, understanding your reactions and choices better. This process often leads to a deeper sense of peace and closure. It's not uncommon to start writing with a particular perception of an event, only to discover new layers of emotions and insights as you delve deeper. Literary creation can be particularly healing if you've experienced challenges you've struggled to understand. By revisiting these through writing, you can often find a way to reconcile with the past and appreciate how far you've come.

When considering sharing your personal stories, whether publicly in a blog or a book or privately in a journal or with close friends, think carefully about what feels right. Sharing your journey can be incredibly empowering and inspire others in their paths. However, ensuring you're comfortable and ready to open up about your experiences is significant. If you choose to share publicly, prepare for a range of responses. While many can be overwhelmingly positive and supportive, there may be criticism, too. Ensure you're emotionally prepared for this, and remember that a few adverse reactions don't diminish your story's worth. If you're more comfortable keeping your writings private, they can remain a personal reminder of your resilience and growth. Alternatively, sharing these stories in a more controlled environment, such as support groups or workshops, can be fulfilling. It allows you to connect with others who might benefit from hearing your experiences while providing a safe space to express yourself.

Using your personal stories to inspire self-love and resilience in others can be one of the most rewarding aspects of sharing your journey. Reading or hearing about someone overcoming difficulties and embracing self-love can ignite hope and motivation in them. Your stories can show that change is possible, that self-love is attainable, and that they are not alone in their struggles. If you're inclined to use your narrative to help others, consider focusing on the aspects of your story that highlight overcoming self-doubt, learning to set boundaries, or finding joy in the small things. These themes are universally relatable and can provide powerful lessons in self-love and resilience. You might also include specific strategies or practices that helped you along the way, providing readers with valuable techniques they can implement daily. These anecdotes make your story inspirational and actionable, which can be very impactful for someone just starting their journey toward self-love.

In sum, writing your self-love journey is more than just recounting your life; it's about uncovering and sharing the essence of your personal growth. Whether kept private or shared, these narratives hold immense power to heal, inspire, and teach, both for you and for others. While you continue crafting and sharing your story, let it be a testament to the beauty of self-discovery and the transformative power of self-love.

8.4 CREATING ART FROM THE HEART: LEAVING A TANGIBLE LEGACY

Art can touch souls and connect hearts in ways words sometimes cannot. It's a universal language transcending age, culture, and time, offering a profound medium to express and share love, insights, and personal revelations. For you, stepping into the world of artistic expression can be a delightful avenue to leave a tangible legacy that carries the essence of your spirit and your journey of self-love and discovery. Whether you've always had an artistic side or are just beginning to explore this part of yourself, creating art can be an impactful experience that uplifts your spirit and forges deep connections with others.

Encouraging yourself to express feelings and experiences through art can be liberating. It's about letting your inner world flow outward, making the invisible feelings within visible. This process can be incredibly therapeutic, helping to process emotions and experiences that are sometimes hard to articulate. You might choose painting to express vibrant emotions or sculpting to work through more tactile, intricate feelings. Or maybe photography captures your eye, where light and shadows play together to tell stories without words. Each stroke, mold, or snapshot is a piece of your heart made visible, a step in your self-exploration.

Using art to connect with others offers a powerful way to share messages of love and empowerment. Art can be a conversation starter, sharing perspectives and inspiring thoughts that might otherwise go unspoken. Consider hosting small art shows within your community or sharing your creations online. These platforms allow you to share pieces of your personal story and the lessons learned along the way. The beauty of sharing art lies in its ability to resonate differently with each viewer, often sparking reflection and personal connections that might not have been possible otherwise. It's about creating those moments of connection that can ripple out, touching others' lives and inspiring them to explore their paths of self-expression and self-love.

Exploring diverse mediums and forms of art can be an exciting part of your artistic journey. If you're new to creating art, start with something simple and accessible, like sketching or watercolor painting. These mediums are forgiving and spontaneous, which might be less intimidating if you're just starting. As you grow more confident, you might delve into more complex mediums like oil painting or digital art, each offering new challenges and ways to express your personality and vision. Remember, the key isn't mastery but expression. It's about finding joy in creation, not just the outcome. Every new medium you try can unlock new avenues of creativity and self-discovery, enriching your journey and adding depth to your legacy of art.

Art as a gift extends the reach of your legacy, turning personal creations into meaningful tokens of love and connection. Consider gifting your artwork on special occasions or just because you want to. A piece of art you make can be a deeply personal and heartfelt present, carrying your energy and affection. For instance, a small painting given to a friend can become a cherished keepsake, a reminder of your relationship and the moments shared. Or a handcrafted pottery item, no matter how simple, can become a daily favorite, infusing routine with significance. These art pieces become more than just objects; they are tangible manifestations of love, crafted by your hands and imagination, meant to be held and appreciated in the daily lives of those you care about.

In embracing art as a part of your life, you open up a world of expression, connection, and legacy. It's a way to visually share your journey, connect deeply with others, and leave tangible tokens of your experiences and insights behind. As you continue to explore and create, let each piece reflect your unique perspective, love, and journey toward deeper self-understanding and expression. Whether through colors, forms, or images, your art is a powerful testament to your life and the love you've cultivated within it.

8.5 THE POWER OF MENTORSHIP: GUIDING OTHERS ON THEIR PATH

Think of when someone took you under their wing, shared their knowledge, and guided you through a rough patch or a steep learning curve. That person was more than just a guide; they were a mentor whose impact shaped your approach to challenges and personal growth. Imagine yourself in those shoes, being the mentor who lights the way for others. Engaging in mentorship is a profoundly fulfilling role that enriches both the mentor's and the mentee's lives, integrating threads of wisdom, experience, and mutual growth while creating connections that extend beyond individual lives and influence the broader society.

Mentorship, especially as you embrace the later chapters of your life, offers an exceptional avenue to share the wealth of wisdom you've accumulated. It's about passing on knowledge, values, and insights on living a life enriched with self-love and purpose. Whether in a professional setting, within your family, or in a volunteer capacity, your life experiences are invaluable. They equip you to guide others through similar challenges and triumphs, providing a roadmap to help them along their paths with greater confidence and fewer stumbles. For instance, mentoring a young professional in your former industry can be super rewarding. You can help them understand not only the technical aspects of the job but also how to handle workplace dynamics and career growth, which they often learn through experience rather than formal education.

The beauty of mentorship lies in its reciprocity. While the mentee learns from your experiences and advice, you gain fresh perspectives and new ideas that can invigorate your own life and thinking. This mutual growth is one of the most rewarding aspects of the mentor-mentee relationship. It keeps your mind sharp and your heart open, reminding you that learning is a lifelong process. Engaging with younger or less experienced individuals can challenge and change your views, leading to a deeper understanding of yourself and the world around you. It's a dynamic interchange where wisdom flows both ways, enriched by each person's unique experiences and insights.

Finding individuals or groups who can benefit from your mentorship might seem daunting, but there may be more opportunities than you initially thought. Start by identifying networks within your community through local clubs, schools, or business associations where your particular skills and experiences can serve best. Many organizations constantly need seasoned professionals who can guide and support newcomers. Additionally, consider online platforms that connect mentors and mentees globally. These platforms can be advantageous if you're looking to expand your impact beyond your local community, reaching out to individuals in different parts of the world who might benefit from your expertise. When choosing who to mentor, look for individuals who show potential and eagerness to learn and share a sense of values and work ethic that align with your own. This alignment can make the mentorship more effective and enjoyable for both parties.

In every mentorship role, the heart of your effort lies in the genuine desire to help others succeed. This desire isn't about merely relaying information or giving advice. It's about inspiring, challenging, and supporting your mentees as they discover and traverse their paths. As you guide them through their professional and personal growth, you reinforce your legacy of love and wisdom, impacting lives in ways that may unfold across generations. So, as you consider stepping into the role of a mentor, remember it's one of the most influential ways to contribute to someone's life, offering a blend of guidance, wisdom, and mutual growth that enriches both your lives.

8.6 LIVING YOUR LEGACY: HOW EVERYDAY ACTIONS REFLECT YOUR LOVE JOURNEY

In our everyday lives, each action, no matter how small, creates a pattern that goes beyond our immediate surroundings, shaping a legacy filled with love, compassion, and growth. The often-overlooked morning smiles, the patient listening during a friend's hard day, and even the self-respect shown when you take a moment for yourself— these actions possess the power to influence and inspire, constructing a legacy that withstands the test of time.

Everyday acts of love are meaningful yet understated ways you contribute to this legacy. Consider how a simple gesture of kindness can alter the course of someone's day. From offering a heartfelt compliment to a co-worker to preparing a favorite meal for your family, these acts of love ripple through your circle of influence, often setting off a chain reaction of positivity. In your community, these gestures build an environment of goodwill and support, where small kindnesses become the norm, not the exception. This ongoing exchange of kindness fosters a community spirit and cements your role as a contributor to its warmth and cohesion.

Consistency in self-love practices is crucial for ensuring these actions aren't just sporadic good deeds but a sustainable part of your lifestyle. By integrating self-love into your daily routine— through affirmations each morning, regular self-reflection, or setting aside time for your passions—you ensure that the care you extend outward is also flowing inward. This consistent replenishment allows you to keep giving without draining your reservoir of energy and compassion. It also sets a powerful example for those around you, showing that caring deeply for oneself is the wellspring from which genuine care for others can flow freely.

Recognizing the domino effect of your actions on others highlights the interconnectedness of your practices and their broader influence. From the words you use to your attitudes, each choice you make can inspire, uplift, and even challenge others to reflect on their behaviors and beliefs. For instance, remaining optimistic and solution-focused in challenging situations can inspire others to adopt a similar outlook, cultivating a more resilient and hopeful community. Similarly, your commitment to personal integrity and ethical behavior can serve as a moral compass for those within your sphere, guiding them through their ethical dilemmas.

Focusing on leaving a legacy that reflects your core values of love, compassion, and growth involves an intentional approach to living each day. It means making choices that align with personal goals and the world you wish to create and leave behind. Whether through environmental stewardship, advocating for justice and equality, or simply living a life of kindness and generosity, each action contributes to a legacy that can endure beyond your years, influencing future generations.

As you continue to build this legacy through your daily actions and decisions, consider how each moment reflects the broader narrative of your life. Whether interacting with a neighbor, making decisions at work, or spending time with family, each scenario is an opportunity to reinforce the values you cherish. You don't build your legacy in a day but rather through accumulating days filled with intentional living. As you move through your days, remember the power you hold in shaping your destiny, shaping the structure of your community, and setting a foundation for future generations.

In wrapping up this chapter, remember that the legacy you leave is crafted daily, not through grand gestures but through consistent acts of love, choices that reflect self-love, and the values you live by. These elements create a resonant story that defines who you are and what you stand for, resonating through your community and echoing into the future. As we turn the page to the next chapter, let's commit to living a life that enriches our soul and empowers and uplifts others, leaving a trail of love and positivity in our wake.

Keeping the Game Alive

Now that you have everything you need to attain unshakeable self-love, radiant happiness, and deeply fulfilling relationships, it's time to pass on your newfound knowledge and show other readers where they can find the same help.

Simply by leaving your honest opinion of this book on Amazon, you'll show other women in their midlives where they can find the information they're looking for and pass their passion for loving themselves forward.

Thank you for your help. Self-love is kept alive when we pass on our knowledge – and you're helping me to do just that.

Scan the QR code below to leave your review on Amazon.

Conclusion

As we come to the end of this journey together, I want to reflect on the transformative power of self-love, especially for us, the dynamic women exploring the diverse landscape of life beyond 50. Throughout our conversation in these pages, we've explored how deeply self-love can enhance our personal growth, happiness, and relationships. From nurturing our bodies and souls, overcoming daily obstacles, and healing from our pasts to cultivating meaningful relationships and gracefully embracing life's transitions— we've explored topics that I hope have planted seeds of change in your life.

Remember, the path to self-love is beautifully iterative. Each small, manageable step you take is a building block in constructing a resilient, joyful life. It's not about reaching a destination but about continuing to layer experiences and insights that enrich your journey. This step-by-step approach ensures that each growth phase is solid, sustainable, and deeply integrated into your being.

As you've turned each page, I hope you've noticed the subtle shifts within yourself—moments of clarity, sparks of joy, or a newfound peace that weren't as pronounced before. These are the signs of your evolving journey, the quiet affirmations that you are moving in the right direction. Be patient and persistent with yourself. One morning, you'll wake up to find that these subtle changes have culminated in a profound transformation, and you'll marvel at how far you've come.

Please take a moment now to reflect on your experience with this book. How have your thoughts, feelings, and behaviors shifted? Recognizing these changes, no matter how small, is integral as it reinforces your commitment to this path and highlights your progress.

As we part ways, I hope you don't see this as an end but a beautiful continuation of your adventure. Keep applying the principles and strategies we've discussed. Allow your life to be an experiment in discovering new ways to deepen self-love. Revisit these pages whenever you need encouragement or a reminder of your journey.

Share your story of transformation and self-love. Whether via social media, writing, or talking with friends and family, your story can inspire and uplift others. Imagine the chain reaction of our collective stories encouraging more and more women to embark on this journey of self-discovery and love.

Lastly, here is my personal note: I am filled with hope and joy for your journey ahead. Remember, you are not alone. You possess everything you need within to design your best life—a life brimming with love, joy, and fulfillment. Keep loving yourself, growing, and shining your unique light on the world.

With all my love and best wishes, Jillian

References

1. VCU Health. (n.d.). Loving yourself and others: The impact of compassion on mental health and wellness. VCU Health. Retrieved from https://www.vcuhealth.org/news/loving-yourself-and-others-the-impact-of-compassion-on-mental-health-and-wellness

2. Honey Good. (n.d.). 9 mindfulness exercises after 50 that you should start. Honey Good. Retrieved from https://www.honeygood.com/mindfulness-exercises-after-50/

3. Baby Boomster. (n.d.). How to stop feeling invisible as a woman over 50. Baby Boomster. Retrieved from https://babyboomster.com/feeling-invisible/

4. BetterHelp. (n.d.). Love gone wrong: Malignant self-love and narcissism. BetterHelp. Retrieved from https://www.betterhelp.com/advice/love/love-gone-wrong-malignant-self-love-and-narcissism/

5. Mayo Clinic News Network. (n.d.). Mayo mindfulness: Overcoming negative self-talk. Mayo Clinic News Network. Retrieved from https://newsnetwork.mayoclinic.org/discussion/mayo-mindfulness-overcoming-negative-self-talk/

6. Content Hacker. (n.d.). Create powerful daily affirmations based on your identity. Content Hacker. Retrieved from https://contenthacker.com/affirmations/

7. BetterUp. (n.d.). Why vulnerability will change your life: The power of vulnerability. BetterUp. Retrieved from https://www.betterup.com/blog/vulnerability

8. The Midlife Whisperer. (n.d.). Overcoming perfectionism with self-compassion. The Midlife Whisperer. Retrieved from https://themidlifewhisperer.com/overcoming-perfectionism-with-self-compassion/

9. Cheers to Chapter Two. (n.d.). Women's health over 50: A holistic approach. Cheers to Chapter Two. Retrieved from https://cheers2chapter2.com/womens-health-over-50-a-holistic-approach

10. PubMed Central (PMC). (n.d.). Can physical activity improve the mental health of older adults? PubMed Central. Retrieved from https://www.ncbi.nlm.nih.gov/pmc/articles/PMC449721/

11. LinkedIn. (n.d.). The role of spirituality in personal growth: How can it help us grow? LinkedIn. Retrieved from https://www.linkedin.com/pulse/role-spirituality-personal-growth-how-can-help-us-grow-akshay-kute-xxvqf

12. Mind. (n.d.). What are arts and creative therapies? Mind. Retrieved from

https://www.mind.org.uk/information-support/drugs-and-treatments/talking-therapy-and-counselling/arts-and-creative-therapies/

13. Life Beyond the Kitchen. (n.d.). Self-care ideas for middle-aged women that you can do today. Life Beyond the Kitchen. Retrieved from https://lifebeyondthekitchen.com/self-care-ideas-for-middle-aged-women-that-you-can-do-today/

14. HelpGuide.org. (n.d.). Setting healthy boundaries in relationships. HelpGuide.org. Retrieved from https://www.helpguide.org/articles/relationships-communication/setting-healthy-boundaries-in-relationships.htm

15. GoodRx. (n.d.). Why a "digital detox" will benefit your overall mental health. GoodRx. Retrieved from https://www.goodrx.com/health-topic/mental-health/digital-detox

16. National Debt Relief. (n.d.). Financial self-love checklist. National Debt Relief. Retrieved from https://www.nationaldebtrelief.com/blog/financial-wellness/financial-education/financial-self-love-checklist/

17. Verywell Mind. (n.d.). How to heal from trauma: 10 strategies that can help. Verywell Mind. Retrieved from https://www.verywellmind.com/10-ways-to-heal-from-trauma-5206940

18. Mayo Clinic. (n.d.). Forgiveness: Letting go of grudges and bitterness. Mayo Clinic. Retrieved from https://www.mayoclinic.org/healthy-lifestyle/adult-health/in-depth/forgiveness/art-20047692

19. Verywell Family. (n.d.). 7 strategies for overcoming empty nest syndrome. Verywell Family. Retrieved from https://www.verywellfamily.com/7-strategies-for-overcoming-empty-nest-syndrome-5180842

20. Healthline. (n.d.). Life after divorce: 12 key steps for moving on. Healthline. Retrieved from https://www.healthline.com/health/life-after-divorce

21. Time. (n.d.). How to set boundaries with your family. Time. Retrieved from https://time.com/6331383/how-to-set-boundaries-family/

22. Verywell Mind. (n.d.). Assertive communication: What it means and how to use it. Verywell Mind. Retrieved from https://www.verywellmind.com/learn-assertive-communication-in-five-simple-steps-3144969

23. Psychology Today. (n.d.). Self-love is the new #RelationshipGoals. Psychology Today. Retrieved from https://www.psychologytoday.com/us/blog/couples-thrive/201906/self-love-is-the-new-relationshipgoals

24. PlusAPN. (n.d.). Overcoming social anxiety: 20 ways to build confidence and connection. PlusAPN. Retrieved from https://plusapn.com/resources/overcoming-social-anxiety-20-ways-to-build-confidence-and-connection/

25. BioMed Central (BMC). (n.d.). Mental health around retirement: Evidence of Ashenfelter's dip. Global Health Research and Policy. Retrieved from https://ghrp.biomedcentral.com/articles/10.1186/s41256-023-00320-3

26. The Telegraph. (n.d.). Over 50s dating tips to find a connection. The Telegraph. Retrieved from https://www.telegraph.co.uk/online-dating/mature-dating/over-50s-dating/

27. U.S. News & World Report. (n.d.). 8 tips for finding a hobby in retirement. U.S. News & World Report. Retrieved from https://money.usnews.com/money/blogs/on-retirement/articles/8-tips-for-finding-a-hobby-in-retirement

28. Raising Children Network. (n.d.). Grandparents: Roles and boundaries. Raising Children Network. Retrieved from https://raisingchildren.net.au/grown-ups/grandparents/family-relationships/roles-boundaries

29. HelpGuide.org. (n.d.). Volunteering and its surprising benefits. HelpGuide.org. Retrieved from https://www.helpguide.org/articles/healthy-living/volunteering-and-its-surprising-benefits.htm

30. Camber Mental Health. (2022, May 26). Five ways to help kids build self-esteem and love themselves. Camber Mental Health. Retrieved from https://www.cambermentalhealth.org/2022/05/26/five-ways-to-help-kids-build-self-esteem-and-love-themselves/

31. PubMed Central (PMC). (n.d.). Writing therapy: A new tool for general practice? PubMed Central. Retrieved from https://www.ncbi.nlm.nih.gov/pmc/articles/PMC3505408/

32. Neal Dempsey. (n.d.). The impact of mentorship on personal and professional development. Neal Dempsey. Retrieved from https://www.nealdempsey.com/blog-posts/the-impact-of-mentorship-on-personal-and-professional-development